# New Daylight

Edited by Sally Welch January–April 2017

**The Bible Reading Fellowship**
15 The Chambers, Vineyard, Abingdon OX14 3FE
Tel: 01865 319700; Fax: 01865 319701
E-mail: enquiries@brf.org.uk; Website: www.brf.org.uk

ISBN 978 0 85746 439 2

Distributed in Australia by Mediacom Education Inc., PO Box 610, Unley, SA 5061.
Tel: 1800 811 311; Fax: 08 8297 8719;
E-mail: admin@mediacom.org.au
Available also from all good Christian bookshops in Australia.
For individual and group subscriptions in Australia:
Mrs Rosemary Morrall, PO Box W35, Wanniassa, ACT 2903.

Distributed in New Zealand by Scripture Union Wholesale, PO Box 760, Wellington
Tel: 04 385 0421; Fax: 04 384 3990; E-mail: suwholesale@clear.net.nz

Publications distributed to more than 60 countries

**Acknowledgments**


Printed by Gutenberg Press, Tarxien, Malta.

# Suggestions for using *New Daylight*

Find a regular time and place, if possible, where you can read and pray undisturbed. Before you begin, take time to be still and perhaps use the BRF prayer. Then read the Bible passage slowly (try reading it aloud if you find it over-familiar), followed by the comment. You can also use *New Daylight* for group study and discussion, if you prefer.

The prayer or point for reflection can be a starting point for your own meditation and prayer. Many people like to keep a journal to record their thoughts about a Bible passage and items for prayer. In *New Daylight* we also note the Sundays and some special festivals from the Church calendar, to keep in step with the Christian year.

# *New Daylight* and the Bible

*New Daylight* contributors use a range of Bible versions, and you will find a list of the versions used opposite, on page 2. You are welcome to use your own preferred version alongside the passage printed in the notes. This can be particularly helpful if the Bible text has been abridged.

*New Daylight* affirms that the whole of the Bible is God's revelation to us, and we should read, reflect on and learn from every part of both Old and New Testaments. Usually the printed comment presents a straightforward 'thought for the day', but sometimes it may also raise questions rather than simply providing answers, as we wrestle with some of the more difficult passages of Scripture.

*New Daylight* is also available in a standard edition (smaller format). Visit your local Christian bookshop or contact the BRF office, who can also give details about a cassette version for the visually impaired. For a Braille edition, contact St John's Guild, Sovereign House, 12–14 Warwick Street, Coventry CV5 6ET.

# Comment on *New Daylight*

To send feedback, you may email or write to BRF at the addresses shown opposite. If you would like your comment to be included on our website, please email connect@brf.org.uk. You can also Tweet to @brfonline (please use the hashtag #brfconnect).

# Writers in this issue

**Fiona Stratta** is a Speech and Language therapist and Speech and Drama teacher. She has written two books: *Walking with Gospel Women* (BRF, 2012) and *Walking with Old Testament Women* (BRF, 2015).

**Naomi Starkey** is a curate in the Church in Wales, working in Welsh and English across six rural churches on the Llyn Peninsula. She has written a number of books, including *The Recovery of Hope* (BRF, 2016) and *The Recovery of Love* (BRF, 2012).

**Andrew Jones** is the Archdeacon of Meirionnydd in the Diocese of Bangor (Wales). He has written *Pilgrimage: The journey to remembering our story* (BRF, 2011) and *Mary: A Gospel witness to transfiguration and liberation* (BRF, 2014).

**John Twisleton** is Rector of St Giles, Horsted Keynes in Sussex. He writes on prayer and apologetics, broadcasts on Premier Radio, and is the author of *Meet Jesus* (BRF, 2011) and *Using the Jesus Prayer* (BRF, 2014).

**Veronica Zundel** is an Oxford graduate, writer and columnist. She lives with her husband and son in north London. Her most recent book is *Everything I Know about God, I've Learned from Being a Parent* (BRF, 2013).

**Steve Aisthorpe** lives in the Highlands of Scotland with his wife and two sons. He works for the Church of Scotland, facilitating retreats, providing training, undertaking research, and helping churches to discern God's future direction.

**David Winter** is retired from parish ministry. An honorary Canon of Christ Church, Oxford, he is well known as a writer and broadcaster. His most recent book for BRF is *Heaven's Morning: Rethinking our destination*.

**Liz Hoare** is an ordained Anglican priest and teaches spiritual formation at Wycliffe Hall, Oxford. Her interests lie in the history and literature of Christian spirituality and their connections with today's world.

**Sally Welch** is a parish priest in the Diocese of Oxford. She has written several books on aspects of adults' and children's spirituality and has a particular interest in pilgrimage and labyrinths.

# Sally Welch writes...

The first issue of a new year is always a privilege to work on, bringing with it a sense of new beginning and including the great festival of Easter, resonant with hope and love. This issue is no exception, and I am delighted that we have such an interesting and challenging selection of contributions, bringing depth to our understanding of the Bible and of the Christian life. The writers come from a variety of backgrounds and offer a range of reflections and learning, but uniting them all is a deep personal faith and a burning desire to share the insights they have gained from prayer, study and reflection.

There is a wonderful mix of subject and approach within this issue—from John Twisleton's careful exploration of the parallels between the Old and the New Testament, which shine a light on God's saving work throughout the history of creation, to Fiona Stratta's presentation of the character of the disciples, whose relationship with Jesus serves as an example for our own. Veronica Zundel's study of different approaches to the doctrine of the atonement is challenging and profound. Some of the interpretations she examines might be unnerving to us; others will strike a deep chord of recognition, but all will help us to understand the complexity of Christ's saving action on the cross. The details of Jesus' last journey, his death and resurrection are explored sensitively and wisely by Liz Hoare, who also examines the implications of his loving sacrifice for each one of us.

The word 'epiphany' derives from the Greek *epiphaneia*, meaning 'revelation' or 'manifestation'. As we move from the church season of Epiphany through Lent to Easter and beyond in the company of such a varied group of personalities, I pray that you will each receive your own epiphany or moment of understanding, and that this moment serves to illuminate the path of your spiritual journey.

*Lord God, you have called your servants to ventures of which we cannot see the ending, by paths as yet untrodden, through perils unknown. Give us faith to go out with good courage, not knowing where we go, but only that your hand is leading us and your love supporting us; through Jesus Christ our Lord. Amen*

LUTHERAN BOOK OF WORSHIP (AUGSBURG FORTRESS PUBLISHING 1978)

## The BRF Prayer

*Almighty God,*
*you have taught us that your word is a lamp for our feet*
*and a light for our path. Help us, and all who prayerfully*
*read your word, to deepen our fellowship with you*
*and with each other through your love.*
*And in so doing may we come to know you more fully,*
*love you more truly, and follow more faithfully*
*in the steps of your son Jesus Christ, who lives and reigns*
*with you and the Holy Spirit, one God for evermore.*
*Amen*

# The twelve disciples

The twelve ordinary men who were to live such extraordinary lives were chosen by Jesus. The word 'disciple' comes from the Latin *discipulus* and means a pupil or student-follower. Disciples learnt the distinctive teaching of their chosen rabbi. The Pharisees had disciples, as did John the Baptist. Jesus, although not trained as a rabbi (John 7:14–15), was popularly considered as one (John 3:1–2).

Jesus had many disciples—he sent out 72 disciples to further his ministry, and many women accompanied him—but the Twelve were chosen for a special purpose, an apostolic mission. An apostle is an ambassador or messenger; the Twelve were to be ambassadors to all the nations, passing on the message given by Jesus: 'Go and make disciples of all the nations, baptising them in the name of the Father and the Son and the Holy Spirit. Teach these new disciples to obey all the commands I have given you. And be sure of this: I am with you always, even to the end of the age' (Matthew 28:19–20, NLT). The disciples were to have a relationship with Jesus that went far beyond that of pupil and teacher. It was to involve not just a way of interpreting the scriptures but a loyalty that took them away from family, business and possessions; it was to be life-transforming.

In the summer of 2015, I visited the Archbasilica of St John Lateran in Rome, where there are stunning larger-than-life statues of the twelve apostles (Judas is replaced by Paul). You may like to look at pictures online. I was moved by the craftsmanship and the statues' beauty. I was intrigued both by the representation of each character and by the events and circumstances in the apostles' lives that the sculptors alluded to in their handiworks. The disciples became individuals to me in a new way. These flawed yet strong men, through the power of the Holy Spirit, were trusted with a message that was to turn the world upside-down.

As we look at each of the disciples in turn, there is much to learn, but perhaps the overriding lesson that the twelve disciples teach us is that Jesus sees not only who we are but also who we can become.

FIONA STRATTA

# Andrew

The following day John was again standing with two of his disciples. As Jesus walked by, John looked at him and declared, 'Look! There is the Lamb of God!' When John's two disciples heard this, they followed Jesus... Andrew, Simon Peter's brother, was one of these men who heard what John said and then followed Jesus. Andrew went to find his brother, Simon, and told him, 'We have found the Messiah' (which means 'Christ').

Andrew, originally a disciple of John the Baptist, came from Bethsaida in Galilee (John 1:44). He was a fisherman with his brother, Simon, and soon both would leave their business to follow Jesus full-time. John 1 tells of Andrew's first meeting with Jesus, when he spent the day with him. In that short space of time, Andrew went from recognising Jesus as a rabbi to being convinced he had found the Messiah. It was to take time, though, for him to realise the full implications of this discovery and the deeper meaning of John the Baptist's name for Jesus—'the Lamb of God'.

Andrew brought people to Jesus—first his brother Simon and later the boy with the loaves and fish, which Jesus used to feed 5000 people (John 6:8–9). Although Andrew was doubtful about how so small an amount of food could feed a crowd ('But what good is that with this huge crowd?' he asked), he still played his part in bringing the boy with his picnic to Jesus' attention. We see faith and doubt constantly intertwined in the narratives concerning the disciples. Often, we too live with doubt and faith running alongside each other, and this may bring a sense of guilt. Andrew shows us that if we bring the little we have and offer it to the Lord, we will be amazed at what he does with it. We, like Andrew, only need to have faith the size of a mustard seed to see mountains being moved.

---

*Andrew brought his brother Simon to Jesus, yet it was Simon who became the most influential of the disciples. Let us pray to be humble like Andrew, the younger brother who stood back and watched Simon take on a key role in God's kingdom.*

FIONA STRATTA

# Simon Peter

Simon Peter answered, 'You are the Messiah, the Son of the living God.' Jesus replied, 'You are blessed, Simon son of John, because my Father in heaven has revealed this to you. You did not learn this from any human being. Now I say to you that you are Peter (which means 'rock'), and upon this rock I will build my church, and all the powers of hell will not conquer it.'

Jesus had great plans for Peter, a natural leader and hence spokesperson for the disciples, but Peter had a lot to learn. He was so quick to speak that he often put his foot in it (Mark 8:32–33). His self-confident actions were at times impulsive (Matthew 14:28–30). However, Jesus used these as learning opportunities not only for Peter but also for the other disciples. For example, when Jesus rescued Peter as he attempted to walk on the water, he challenged Peter's lack of faith. The episode, a seeming failure from Peter's perspective, caused the other disciples to be so amazed at all they had seen that they worshipped Jesus through fresh eyes, exclaiming, 'You really are the Son of God' (Matthew 14:33).

Peter had to learn humility and be broken in order to become the servant-hearted leader whom we meet in his letters. His breaking-point came when he realised that, just as Jesus had predicted, he had denied the Lord three times; his claim that he would die with Jesus had come to nothing (Luke 22:54–62). In spite of this, Jesus made a special appearance to Peter after the resurrection (Luke 24:34). We do not know the details of this first reunion, but we can read how Simon Peter was given three opportunities to reaffirm his love for Christ and his commitment to building the church (John 21:15–17). Peter's natural gifts—his leadership, courage and passion—were to become supernaturally used, as, emboldened by the Holy Spirit, he became the rock on which the church was built.

---

*Pray using Peter's words: 'Lord, to whom would we go? You have the words that give eternal life. We believe, and we know you are the Holy One of God' (John 6:68–69).*

FIONA STRATTA

# Philip

The next day Jesus decided to go to Galilee. He found Philip and said to him, 'Come, follow me.' Philip was from Bethsaida, Andrew and Peter's hometown. Philip went to look for Nathanael and told him, 'We have found the very person Moses and the prophets wrote about! His name is Jesus, the son of Joseph from Nazareth.'...

Jesus... saw a huge crowd of people coming to look for him. Turning to Philip, he asked, 'Where can we buy bread to feed all these people?' He was testing Philip, for he already knew what he was going to do. Philip replied, 'Even if we worked for months, we wouldn't have enough money to feed them!'

It is likely that Andrew, Peter, James, John, Philip and Nathanael were young men who had known each other for some years and that there were close friendships among them. Philip, like Andrew, was quick to recognise Jesus as the long-awaited Messiah, and his understanding would continue to grow.

In the story of the feeding of the 5000, we read how Jesus tested Philip. From answering Jesus' question, Philip gained self-knowledge—an insight into the measure of faith he had developed (or not developed) during the time that they had spent together. Jesus' overarching goal was to develop Philip's faith further. It seems, from Philip's reply, that he did not pass the test, for in spite of the miracles he had already witnessed, he viewed the problem with the hungry crowd as insoluble. We so often respond similarly: we have seen the Lord provide for us and for others, and yet, when the new challenge comes, we find ourselves wondering how on earth the problem can be resolved. Meanwhile, in heaven our Lord already knows how he will provide, whether through a miracle or by giving us grace to endure, even to thrive inwardly.

---

*Shortly before Jesus' death, Philip asked him, 'Lord, show us the Father.' Jesus' reply contained a challenge and an encouragement: 'Have I been with you all this time, Philip, and yet you still don't know who I am? Anyone who has seen me has seen the Father' (John 14:8–9). Thank God for his revelation in Jesus.*

FIONA STRATTA

# Nathanael

'Nazareth!' exclaimed Nathanael. 'Can anything good come from Nazareth?' 'Come and see for yourself.' Philip replied. As they approached, Jesus said, 'Now here is a genuine son of Israel—a man of complete integrity.' 'How do you know about me?' Nathanael asked. Jesus replied, 'I could see you under the fig tree before Philip found you.' Then Nathanael exclaimed, 'Rabbi, you are the Son of God, the King of Israel!'

Nathanael was Philip's friend from Cana (John 21:2). His name also occurs as Bartholomew (a surname) alongside Philip's (Matthew 10:3). When Philip told Nathanael about Jesus, Nathanael's initial response was sceptical, for Nazareth, a Roman garrison four miles from Cana, was an insignificant town of poor reputation. Nathanael, as a 'son of Israel', knew that the Messiah was to come from Bethlehem in Judea (Micah 5:2). Philip wisely suggested that Nathanael meet Jesus for himself, and, on the strength of their friendship, Nathanael agreed.

Like Philip, we can share our spiritual journey, but each individual needs their own encounter with Jesus in order to make the claim that Nathanael made: 'You are the Son of God—the King of Israel.' Jesus recognised that Nathanael had integrity, a pure heart—the quality of a true Israelite (Psalm 73:1). It is the pure in heart, we learn from the Sermon on the Mount, who will see God. Nathanael's integrity prepared him for the revelation: he had found the Christ, the anointed one who would lead and save Israel.

Like the other disciples', Nathanael's understanding of how this would happen was to be radically altered. Jesus promised Nathanael that he would witness far greater things than Jesus' knowledge of his whereabouts, for he would 'see heaven open and the angels of God going up and down on the Son of Man' (John 1:51). 'Son of Man' was a title that Jesus used frequently to refer to himself; it is found first in Daniel's vision describing the one whose rule would be eternal (Daniel 7:13–14).

*Lord, may we have Nathanael's searching mind and pure heart. Grant us an ever-deepening revelation of you. Amen*

FIONA STRATTA

# John

Standing near the cross were Jesus' mother, and his mother's sister, Mary (the wife of Clopas), and Mary Magdalene. When Jesus saw his mother standing there beside the disciple he loved, he said to her, 'Dear woman, here is your son.' And he said to this disciple, 'Here is your mother.' And from then on this disciple took her into his home.

John's Gospel indicates that John was the closest disciple to Jesus, as the author refers to himself on several occasions as 'the disciple whom Jesus loved'. Their bond must have been very strong, for Jesus entrusted his mother not to his own brothers, but to John. John seems to have taken this role very seriously; Mary was with him in Jerusalem while they waited for the coming of the Holy Spirit (Acts 1:13–14). He understood that his calling was to care, and, although he was involved in the leadership of the Jerusalem church, he does not seem to have had Peter's and Paul's travelling ministry. Rather, he developed a passionate father's heart for the church.

John's character was such that Jesus nicknamed him and his brother the 'Sons of Thunder' (Mark 3:17). This explosive and self-seeking man (Luke 9:54; Mark 10:35–37) discovered just how much he was accepted and loved by Jesus. John wrote, 'God is love, and all who live in love live in God, and God lives in them. And as we live in God, our love grows more perfect... We love each other because he loved us first' (1 John 4:16–17, 19).

The transforming love of Jesus radiates through John's Gospel and letters, written between AD85 and 90, by which time John was probably the only survivor of the first twelve disciples. During the persecution of AD90–95 he was exiled to the island of Patmos and there received the vision of the final triumph of the glorified Christ, recorded in the book of Revelation.

---

*'May you have the power to understand... how wide, how long, how high, and how deep his love is. May you experience the love of Christ... Then you will be made complete with all the fullness of life and power that comes from God' (Ephesians 3:18–19).*

FIONA STRATTA

# James the greater

A little farther up the shore Jesus saw Zebedee's sons, James and John, in a boat repairing their nets. He called them at once, and they also followed him, leaving their father, Zebedee, in the boat with the hired men.

James was probably the elder of Zebedee's two sons as his name always appears before John's. They fished together in their father's successful business and often worked alongside Peter and Andrew. Their mother, Salome, became one of the women who accompanied and supported Jesus' ministry. Peter, James and John together were the inner circle of the disciples: they witnessed the raising of Jairus' daughter (Luke 8:51), the transfiguration (Luke 9:28) and Jesus' agony in the garden of Gethsemane (Mark 14:33).

James and John were passionate but their enthusiasm was sometimes misdirected, and they misunderstood the heart of Jesus' ministry. For example, they wished to call down fire on a Samaritan village that had not welcomed Jesus, although Jesus had previously instructed them not to retaliate but to move on from places where they were not made welcome (Luke 9:5, 54).

Further into Jesus' ministry, he explained to them that suffering lay ahead for him, but James and John still asked Jesus if they could sit at his right and left side in his kingdom (Mark 10:37). Jesus used their error as an opportunity to teach the disciples about servant-leadership, which he had modelled and would continue to model to them. Jesus asked James and John whether they would be prepared to suffer with him. Full of confidence, they assured him that they would—but they later deserted him (Matthew 26:56).

After the resurrection and the filling of the Holy Spirit, James continued to be outspoken, but he spoke about Christ: his selfish ambition had gone. He was the first of the apostles to be killed (around AD44) under the instruction of King Herod Agrippa (Acts 12:2).

---

*Like James and John, we too can learn from our mistakes and grow in spiritual understanding.*

FIONA STRATTA

# Matthew

As Jesus left the town, he saw a tax collector named Levi sitting at his tax collector's booth. 'Follow me and be my disciple,' Jesus said to him. So Levi got up, left everything, and followed him. Later, Levi held a banquet in his home with Jesus as the guest of honour... But the Pharisees and their teachers of religious law complained bitterly... Jesus answered them, 'Healthy people don't need a doctor—sick people do. I have come to call not those who think they are righteous, but those who know they are sinners and need to repent.'

Levi, also known as Matthew (Matthew 9:9) worked in Capernaum as a tax collector, a collaborator with the Romans. He was unpopular with his own people, not least because, like most tax collectors at the time, he would take more commission than was his due. It is likely that he would have known Jesus and have seen miracles before the decisive moment when he gave up everything to follow the Lord. For Matthew, there would be no fishing to return to, no Plan B.

Matthew's celebratory banquet guest list included the disciples and many social outcasts, which bitterly offended the Pharisees. However, Jesus' answer to them shows that he had seen Matthew's heart. Matthew knew his life was at odds with God's purposes; he knew he needed to repent—to turn around—and in doing so he experienced great joy. Jesus' loving mentoring would further transform Matthew, whereas the Pharisees' hypocrisy and hardness of heart prevented them from changing.

God was able to do much through Matthew's softened heart, through both his natural and learned abilities. As a tax collector, Matthew would have known both Greek and Aramaic, probably being Jesus' most literate disciple. He would have been an accurate record keeper and therefore in a strong position to record an account of the life of Jesus. His Gospel contains more than 50 references to Old Testament prophecies pointing to Jesus as the Messiah.

---

*Our natural abilities are of value in building the kingdom of God, but our hearts, like Matthew's, need to be softened in order to 'act justly and to love mercy and to walk humbly' with God (Micah 6:8, NIV).*

FIONA STRATTA

# Thomas

Eight days later the disciples were together again, and this time Thomas was with them. The doors were locked; but suddenly, as before, Jesus was standing among them. 'Peace be with you,' he said. Then he said to Thomas, 'Put your finger here, and look at my hands. Put your hand into the wound in my side. Don't be faithless any longer. Believe!' 'My Lord and my God!' Thomas exclaimed. Then Jesus told him, 'You believe because you have seen me. Blessed are those who believe without seeing me.'

From the few times that Thomas is mentioned in the Gospels (John 11:16; 14:4–6), we can see that he was courageous (John 11:16), and he was a practical man who asked searching questions: 'We have no idea where you are going, so how can we know the way?' (John 14:4–6). However, his most well-known appearance occurs after he has expressed his inability to believe, from a rational perspective, that the other disciples have seen the resurrected Jesus. Whatever he thought of their encounter (perhaps he assumed it was a shared hallucination caused by stress and strain), and in spite of his doubts, Thomas was there with them a week later. Jesus responded to Thomas' frankness, as he had done to his questions in the past, and personal faith rose within Thomas: '*My* Lord and *my* God!'

Jesus then spoke of future believers: 'Blessed are those who believe without seeing me.' Jesus had explained during the last supper that it was better for the disciples that he should go away, for his departure would be followed by the sending of the 'Paraclete'—the advocate, comforter, encourager and counsellor (John 14:16–18). On earth, Jesus could only be in one place at a time; through the Holy Spirit, his ministry would carry on in many different places simultaneously. The Holy Spirit would lead the disciples into all truth, and this fullness of the Spirit would come only after Jesus had returned to the Father.

---

*We are blessed to live after the resurrection and after Pentecost. Jesus promised that those who believe in him could 'ask anything in my name, and I will do it, so that the Son can bring glory to the Father' (John 14:12–13).*

FIONA STRATTA

# James the Younger and Simon the Zealot

One day soon afterward Jesus went up on a mountain to pray, and he prayed to God all night. At daybreak he called together all of his disciples and chose twelve of them to be apostles. Here are their names: Simon (whom he named Peter), Andrew (Peter's brother), James, John, Philip, Bartholomew, Matthew, Thomas, James (son of Alphaeus), Simon (who was called the zealot), Judas (son of James), Judas Iscariot (who later betrayed him). When they came down the mountain, the disciples stood with Jesus on a large, level area, surrounded by many of his followers and by the crowds.

Although we have no details about James, son of Alphaeus, it seems that his mother was one of the women who accompanied Jesus. In Mark 15:40 we read that Mary, mother of James the younger and of Joseph, was with Salome and Mary Magdalene at the crucifixion. These three women went to buy spices to anoint Jesus' body; they were the ones to find that the stone had been rolled away, to hear the words of the angel (Mark 16:1–6) and eventually to tell Peter and the other disciples (Luke 24:10). James and his mother shared a love for the Lord.

The word 'zealot' could refer to Simon's political allegiance. The zealots were fanatical nationalists who wished to drive out the Romans and cause political unrest in whatever way they could. Josephus, the Jewish historian, records their motto: 'No king but the Messiah, no tax but the temple tax and no friend but the zealots'. If Simon was one of the zealots, he would have been at the opposite end of the political spectrum to Matthew. He would have expected Jesus, as the Messiah, to become a powerful political or military leader.

Alternatively, the word 'zealot' could allude to Simon's zeal for religious faith and observance. Whatever our understanding, Simon was clearly a man of passion, and Jesus saw the potential in this quality if it was channelled in the right direction. We are encouraged not to be lukewarm but to have zeal for God.

---

*Lord, give us zeal: may we love the Lord our God with all our heart, all our soul, all our mind and all our strength. Amen*

FIONA STRATTA

# Judas son of James (or Thaddaeus)

Judas (not Judas Iscariot, but the other disciple with that name) said to him, 'Lord, why are you going to reveal yourself only to us and not to the world at large?' Jesus replied, 'All who love me will do what I say. My Father will love them, and we will come and make our home with each of them... I am leaving you with a gift—peace of mind and heart. And the peace I give is a gift the world cannot give. So don't be troubled or afraid... I am going away, but I will come back to you again... I have told you these things before they happen so that when they do happen, you will believe.'

Judas is called Thaddaeus (a surname) in Matthew's and Luke's Gospels, probably to distinguish him from Judas Iscariot. John 14:22 gives us the only recorded words of Judas Thaddaeus. The setting was the last supper, and Jesus had been reassuring the disciples that he would not abandon them. Judas' question indicates that he was still expecting a Messiah to establish an earthly kingdom which would overthrow Rome. This could not happen if Jesus was never going to reveal himself to the rest of the world. What was the point, he reasoned, of Jesus revealing himself only to his disciples?

Jesus' reply to Judas is full of promise and reassurance: the Father who has sent him will also send the Spirit; he will help them remember all that Jesus explained, and will never leave them. Even as Jesus approaches his death, his love and concern are for the disciples; he wants them to believe and not fear when he is taken from them.

We know from scripture that the disciples did not make sense of what Jesus had said until after the resurrection, so his words were of no comfort beforehand. Instead, they suffered great anguish, fear and disillusionment. They abandoned their Lord, watched his crucifixion from a distance, and hid behind locked doors.

How much suffering could we save ourselves if we fully trusted God? How much fear could be alleviated?

---

*Lord, 'I do believe, but help me overcome my unbelief!' (Mark 9:24). Grant me peace of mind and heart. Amen*

FIONA STRATTA

# Judas Iscariot

Then Mary took a twelve-ounce jar of expensive perfume... and she anointed Jesus' feet with it... But Judas Iscariot, the disciple who would soon betray him, said, 'That perfume was worth a year's wages. It should have been sold and the money given to the poor.' Not that he cared for the poor—he was a thief, and since he was in charge of the disciples' money, he often stole some for himself. Jesus replied, 'Leave her alone. She did this in preparation for my burial. You will always have the poor among you, but you will not always have me.'

Judas, son of Simon Iscariot, was chosen by Jesus; he was sent out with the other disciples, and was given power and authority to cast out demons, heal diseases and preach about the kingdom of God (Luke 9:1–2). Before Matthias was chosen as a replacement apostle, Peter said of Judas that he 'was one of us and shared in the ministry with us' (Acts 1:17). Judas witnessed the miracles, heard Jesus' teaching and yet never truly received him. Jesus warned that not all who call him 'Lord' and perform miracles in his name will enter the kingdom of God. The fruit of our lives is the sign of true discipleship.

Judas' life had become a lie. Perhaps Mary's anointing of Jesus' feet was the final straw for him, for, while the other disciples could take Jesus' words of reprimand, it seems that Judas could not. He started looking for a way to betray Jesus to the Jewish authorities.

Jesus warned that he would be betrayed by one of the disciples; at the last supper he made it clear that he knew it would be Judas. He chose to give himself up when Judas betrayed him, following his Father's will, and still greeted Judas at that moment with the words 'My friend' (Matthew 26:50). Perhaps these loving words could have given Judas hope, but his remorse led to suicide rather than to repentance.

The Gospels, Matthew's in particular, make it clear that all the events surrounding Jesus' death had been prophesied and were part of God's plan for salvation. God was in control.

---

*The worst of Jesus' experiences—betrayal, desertion and abandonment—gave us 'life by the power of his name' (John 20:31).*

FIONA STRATTA

# The Messiah, the suffering servant

Then [Jesus] asked them, 'But who do you say I am?' Peter replied, 'You are the Messiah.' But Jesus warned them not to tell anyone about him. Then Jesus began to tell them that the Son of Man must suffer many terrible things and be rejected by the elders, the leading priests, and the teachers of religious law. He would be killed, but three days later he would rise from the dead.

For three years this disparate group of men had watched Jesus' miracles and listened to his teaching; Jesus had puzzled and astonished them. We have seen that the Twelve were disciplined, encouraged and unconditionally loved by him. Initially Jesus did not teach them about his death and resurrection, as these ideas would have been totally beyond their comprehension. While they understood that the Messiah was to 'bring good news to the poor', 'comfort the brokenhearted' and 'proclaim that captives will be released' (Isaiah 61:1–2), they still thought that the Messiah would be a revolutionary hero and rescuer. The disciples certainly did not want to hear of Jesus' suffering. Peter tried to prevent him speaking in this way, for which Jesus had to challenge him: 'You are seeing things merely from a human point of view, not from God's' (Mark 8:33). They were yet to grasp that the Messiah was the suffering servant described in Old Testament scriptures such as Psalm 22 and Isaiah 53.

John 20:8–9 tells us that John ('the disciple who had reached the tomb first') was the first of the Twelve to believe in the resurrection, but he still did not see how the scriptures pointed to it. Jesus' words were only just beginning to become clear.

*Father, like the disciples, we can close ourselves to what we do not want to hear; we can be slow to change a mindset and see a new perspective with all its possibilities. Give us grace to see things from your viewpoint. Amen*

FIONA STRATTA

# The disciples understand

Then [Jesus] said, 'When I was with you before, I told you that everything written about me in the law of Moses and the prophets and in the Psalms must be fulfilled.' Then he opened their minds to understand the Scriptures. And he said, 'Yes, it was written long ago that the Messiah would suffer and die and rise from the dead on the third day. It was also written that this message would be proclaimed in the authority of his name to all the nations, beginning in Jerusalem: "There is forgiveness of sins for all who repent." You are witnesses of all these things. And now I will send the Holy Spirit, just as my Father promised. But stay here in the city until the Holy Spirit comes and fills you with power from heaven.'

Jesus taught, 'Whoever wants to be first must... be the servant of everyone else' (Mark 9:35); then he demonstrated it by washing his disciples' feet. 'Do not judge others,' he instructed (Matthew 7:1), and then showed mercy to the outcasts. 'If any of you wants to be my follower, you must... take up your cross,' he taught (Mark 8:34), and took up *his* cross. 'There is no greater love than to lay down one's life for one's friends,' he declared (John 15:13), and gave up his life. It looked to the disciples as if this was the end, but really it was a new beginning.

When the resurrected Jesus appeared to them, it seemed too good to be true: 'Still they stood there in disbelief, filled with joy and wonder' (Luke 24:41). Having calmed their fears, Jesus opened the disciples' minds to the scriptures. What a moment it must have been when all that Jesus had taught them finally made sense! The message of repentance preached by John the Baptist would continue, but now forgiveness of sins would come through the death of Christ; baptism would be not only by water but by the Holy Spirit. The resurrection and Pentecost changed the men who had deserted Jesus and hidden in fear into the bold men we read about in the book of Acts.

---

*Lord, like the disciples, we know that apart from you we can do nothing. May we be continually dependent on the Holy Spirit. Amen*

FIONA STRATTA

# Endings and new beginnings

Jesus replied, 'Now the time has come for the Son of Man to enter into his glory. I tell you the truth, unless a kernel of wheat is planted in the soil and dies, it remains alone. But its death will produce many new kernels—a plentiful harvest of new lives. Those who love their life in this world will lose it. Those who care nothing for their life in this world will keep it for eternity. Anyone who wants to serve me must follow me.'

In the early chapters of Acts, we witness the transformation of the disciples and the power of the Holy Spirit working through them. Yet there was still more to learn, and more pressures and frictions to resolve. Although Peter preached that salvation and the Holy Spirit were available to all people (Acts 2:17, 21), this knowledge needed to move from his head to his heart. The vision that he received from God and his meeting with the God-fearing Gentile, Cornelius, resulted in this transformation of the heart (Acts 10 and 11). Peter said, 'I see very clearly that God shows no favouritism. In every nation he accepts those who fear him and do what is right' (10:34–35); and, 'Since God gave these Gentiles the same gift he gave us when we believed in the Lord Jesus Christ, who was I to stand in God's way?' (11:17).

We could finish at this glorious moment, but, to complete the story of the first disciples' lives, we should consider the words of John 12:23–26. It is believed that all the apostles except John died as martyrs for their faith. As they attempted to escape persecution, they spread the good news of Christ far afield—in Asia, India, the Middle East and Europe—the Roman empire having opened up the possibility of travel on a wider scale than ever before. They were willing to be kernels of wheat that, in dying, produced many new kernels—a 'harvest of new lives'. Just a handful of seeds started a harvest that has continued throughout the world and down the generations.

---

*Lord, like the disciples, may we continue to be changed into your likeness and be prepared to follow in your footsteps. May we embrace your discipleship. Amen*

FIONA STRATTA

# My favourite scriptures

I had a Bible-based childhood, in which weekly Sunday school and annual summer camps made a major feature of 'memory verses', the learning by heart of selected short Bible passages. These could then be repeated to win prizes, an activity that combined brain training with spiritual nourishment and a welcome supply of book tokens for the successful. The downside of this approach was that it tended to develop a patchwork knowledge of the Bible, focusing on consoling or challenging 'soundbites' with little if any sense of their setting.

A degree in English literature helped bring home to me the importance of context for understanding the meaning and significance of a passage. Later years of editing for BRF provided plenty of hands-on training in maintaining the balance between getting to the heart of a biblical book, which often involved choosing 'highlights', and providing a sufficiently thorough framework for study, offering background information as well as explaining the place of those 'highlights' within the wider story.

I have found it a challenge, then, to choose just 14 readings of the right length and style to offer devotional reading. As I mention on 25 January, for example, I would love to have been able to include the whole of Romans! The beauty of some Old Testament books, such as Ecclesiastes, emerges as much through the slow unfolding of poetic imagery as through the impact of a few verses. As I thought about how to choose my favourite bits of the Bible, though, I realised that at different points of my life, different passages have jumped off the page and straight into my heart, connecting directly with the situation I happened to be in. At other times, friends have drawn my attention to Bible verses or simply mentioned images (such as 'Ebenezer stones') that stayed with me, linking up with ideas that I was already pondering.

Over the next two weeks, I invite you to reflect with me on some of those passages. Writing about them has reminded me of God's faithful care of me through the highs and lows of life, and has encouraged me to continue to trust him for the days that lie ahead.

NAOMI STARKEY

# Setting reminders

While Samuel was sacrificing the burnt offering, the Philistines drew near to engage Israel in battle. But that day the Lord thundered with loud thunder against the Philistines and threw them into such a panic that they were routed before the Israelites. The men of Israel rushed out of Mizpah and pursued the Philistines, slaughtering them along the way to a point below Beth Kar. Then Samuel took a stone and set it up between Mizpah and Shen. He named it Ebenezer, saying, 'Thus far the Lord has helped us.'

Words such as 'slaughter' and 'rout' can make this a hard passage to read in a devotional context, with its flavour of 'God on our side (and not on yours)'. In my years as *New Daylight* editor, I remember making a point repeatedly, not least in letters to readers, that individual scripture portions have to be read in the light of the Bible as a whole. As the overall message of the Bible is not 'God will help us to kill those whom we count our enemies', we must ensure that we read passages such as today's in search of wider meaning.

The detail I would like to highlight here is the stone placed by Samuel to mark the victory. The Hebrew *eben-ezer* means 'stone of help', and a place of that name is also mentioned in 1 Samuel 4:1 and 5:1. Like many other biblical places (such as Carmel, Nebo and Zion), it has been used to name chapels, in contrast to the saints commemorated in most church names.

In my experience, it is lamentably easy to forget the ways in which God has helped us. We bring our needs before him, day by day, and (all being well) give thanks for prayers answered. How often, though, do we consciously bring to mind times of deliverance, times that we could venture to describe as victory, when God reached out to rescue us, even from situations where catastrophe was of our own making? In what ways can we place 'Ebenezer stones' in our lives, so that when we look on them, we are reminded again of all that God has done for us?

---

*Lord, help me to be mindful of your constant saving power.*

NAOMI STARKEY

# Waiting for the Lord

[Elijah] travelled for forty days and forty nights until he reached Horeb, the mountain of God. There he went into a cave and spent the night. And the word of the Lord came to him: 'What are you doing here, Elijah?' He replied, 'I have been very zealous for the Lord God Almighty. The Israelites have rejected your covenant, torn down your altars, and put your prophets to death with the sword. I am the only one left, and now they are trying to kill me too.' The Lord said, 'Go out and stand on the mountain in the presence of the Lord, for the Lord is about to pass by.'

The prophet Elijah ranks among the most colourful characters in the Bible, but his mighty deeds against the dastardly prophets of Baal and wicked King Ahab are balanced by truly human moments such as the one in the passage above. Elijah is close to burnout and breakdown. He has given everything in God's service and has now retreated to a cave on 'the mountain of God'.

To speak of having 'cave time' is a contemporary way of saying, 'I need some time apart, space for reflection.' Elijah hides in the cave from the near-impossible demands of his ministry—but then he hears God's voice, asking, 'Elijah, what are you doing here?' Is the question asked angrily? It appears not, and of course God knows the answer anyway. But still he asks—and asks for Elijah's sake. Elijah needs to reflect, to see that God cares, that God understands, and that he is not condemned for his fears.

We may feel that God's demands are too heavy, that we have nothing left to give, that the darkness and solitude of a cave is the only place where we can survive. There, waiting in the darkness and solitude, we should remember that God cares for us, God understands, and God does not condemn us for our fears. Then, like Elijah, we can wait to hear God speak again: 'I am coming. Go to the cave entrance and wait for me. And you will know what to do.'

---

*Lord God Almighty, come and speak to me, your servant,*
*and renew my strength for your work.*

NAOMI STARKEY

# Running God's way

I am laid low in the dust; preserve my life according to your word. I gave an account of my ways and you answered me; teach me your decrees. Cause me to understand the way of your precepts, that I may meditate on your wonderful deeds. My soul is weary with sorrow; strengthen me according to your word. Keep me from deceitful ways; be gracious to me and teach me your law. I have chosen the way of faithfulness; I have set my heart on your laws. I hold fast to your statutes, Lord; do not let me be put to shame. I run in the path of your commands, for you have broadened my understanding.

I first came across these verses as a sixth-former. After the break-up of what should never be dismissed as a 'teenage romance' (break-ups hurt, however young or old you are), I was leafing through my Bible for consolation and found the final words of this passage leaping out at me, like a promise of hope. No matter how conflicted and despairing I was feeling, no matter how dark and miserable the future now looked, I found encouragement here that following God's way could provide a route out of my distress. What's more, following that way could mean more than stumbling along, making my way as best I could; the psalmist spoke of *running* 'in the path of your commands'. I enjoyed running (I still do) and that image resonated with me at a deep level.

I didn't realise till years later that Psalm 119 is an acrostic psalm, each section starting with a different letter of the Hebrew alphabet. I also didn't realise that its focus is the psalmist's delight in God's law—something that I had assumed was a purely negative 'old covenant', which Jesus came to free us from. Appreciating the craft and original context of the passage literally 'broadened my understanding'. It also challenged me to acknowledge that following 'the way of faithfulness' meant discerning and being obedient to heaven's agenda rather than expecting God to fit in with my plans.

---

*Lord God, I ask that today you would broaden my understanding of what it means to walk your way.*

NAOMI STARKEY

# Hoping for harvest

When the Lord restored the fortunes of Zion, we were like those who dreamed. Our mouths were filled with laughter, our tongues with shouts of joy. Then it was said among the nations, 'The Lord has done great things for them.' The Lord has done great things for us, and we are filled with joy. Restore our fortunes, Lord, like streams in the Negev. Those who sow with tears will reap with songs of joy. Those who go out weeping, carrying seed to sow, will return with songs of joy, carrying sheaves with them.

I love the ecstatic tone of this psalm, the way that astonished happiness glows through the imagery of dreams coming true, deserts streaming with water, and harvest when hope had more or less gone. The Lord is addressed with confidence, as one who has already restored the fortunes of his people. That which he has already done, beyond all expectation, he will do again. The context is the Babylonian exile of the sixth century BC, that most calamitous of events for the chosen people. Here, however, it sounds as if exile has become homecoming. In rescuing and blessing 'Zion' (a name often used to designate Jerusalem), not only has God filled the nation with joy, he has also made it an international byword for divine protection.

Given the mood of joyful energy, we may ignore the detail of the sowing and harvesting image—but it is worth pondering. Picture the group of sowers, breath coming in sobs as they lug out the seed to scatter on the fields. Sowing in a land ravaged by conquering armies would be a foolhardy venture, and they do so with despair rather than much expectation that anything will sprout, let alone grow into crops of any substance. Imagine the following weeks, as the sowers anxiously watch the weather, scan the horizon for attack, and check again and again to see if green shoots are appearing. Finally, weeping turns to singing and, when the time for harvest comes, empty arms are filled with 'sheaves'. Faith is rewarded with fruitfulness.

*Grant me, O God, the courage to plant for a harvest, no matter how unfruitful the outlook appears.*

NAOMI STARKEY

# Remembering God

Remember your Creator in the days of your youth, before the days of trouble come and the years approach when you will say, 'I find no pleasure in them'... Remember him—before the silver cord is severed, and the golden bowl is broken; before the pitcher is shattered at the spring, and the wheel broken at the well, and the dust returns to the ground is came from, and the spirit returns to God who gave it.

Ecclesiastes is a bleak, beautiful book, which is sometimes exactly what you need to read when life feels hard, dreary or simply inexplicable. Best-known for the 'time to be born and a time to die' verses (3:1–8), it circles around the question of life's meaning and purpose, trying and discarding various received wisdoms before coming to an end without any clear sense of conclusion or resolution.

The poetic imagery in today's passage conveys change and decay, even if it is hard to work out exactly what the individual elements signify. The overall message comes through to us urgently in the opening words: 'Remember your Creator now, while you have the energy to do so. Don't leave it too late.' This message ties in with the trajectory of the book as a whole—the quest for meaning, which returns, again and again, to the importance of maintaining a relationship with God. Not that such a relationship does away with the quest; rather, it gives it a grounding and context. God, we must remember, is interested in the whole of our lives, not just deathbed conversions.

We may continue to ponder our own significance and the purpose of our days for as long as those days last—but if we do so as we walk step by step with our maker and redeemer, we can have assurance that there is purpose, that we do have significance, even if the details remain unclear for a frighteningly lengthy time. In my experience, turning away from God in frustration at unanswered questions and apparently unheard prayers may relieve my feelings in the short term, but does not provide a long-term solution.

---

*Creator God, you have made me and you love me.*
*Grant me always to have the energy to seek you.*

NAOMI STARKEY

# Singing in springtime

My beloved spoke and said to me, 'Arise, my darling, my beautiful one, come with me. See! The winter is past; the rains are over and gone. Flowers appear on the earth; the season of singing has come, the cooing of doves is heard in our land. The fig-tree forms its early fruit; the blossoming vines spread their fragrance. Arise, come, my darling; my beautiful one, come with me.'

The theme of restoration runs throughout the Bible. While in Genesis we begin with the story of paradise despoiled through human wrongdoing, what we find repeatedly thereafter is the promise that God will intervene to heal the damage, sort out right from wrong, and establish his rule so visibly that none will be able to deny its authority. In the Old Testament prophets and Psalms, this theme is often linked to the return of the Jewish exiles from Babylon, while in the New Testament what tends to be in view is the second coming, the return of Jesus Christ 'on the clouds of heaven' (Matthew 26:64; Mark 14:62).

Our passage today, a lovely extract from the lovely Song of Songs, speaks of restoration on a more intimate scale. The turning of the season from winter to spring mirrors the blossoming of the relationship between Lover and Beloved, a relationship that down the centuries has been read as a picture of the relationship between Christ and the Church (as elaborated in, for example, the poetry of the 16th-century Spanish mystic St John of the Cross). Whether we read it as portraying love human or divine, the poetry conveys something of paradise restored, of the lost abundance of Eden renewed, where man and woman once walked with God in companionship and harmony.

We should remember that although the biblical account of humanity tells of their fall from grace, the final trajectory is always towards healing and redemption. However heavy the winter rains, one day they will come to an end. However barren the earth, one day green shoots will appear. However bleak the future may appear, one day the world will be made new.

*Lord God, give me grace to endure winter for a season, in the certain hope that spring will come again.*

NAOMI STARKEY

# Seeing the light

The people walking in darkness have seen a great light; on those living in the land of deep darkness a light has dawned... For to us a child is born, to us a son is given, and the government will be on his shoulders. And he will be called Wonderful Counsellor, Mighty God, Everlasting Father, Prince of Peace. Of the greatness of his government and peace there will be no end. He will reign on David's throne and over his kingdom, establishing and upholding it with justice and righteousness from that time on and for ever. The zeal of the Lord Almighty will accomplish this.

This is one of my favourites among the traditional carol service readings. In countries of the northern hemisphere, Christmas falls at the darkest time of year and so the idea of 'light in darkness' has a strong appeal. Living as I do in a remote corner of north Wales, I particularly appreciate the Christmas lights that decorate shops and homes, cheering up the long December evenings. I also appreciate the way that even a small light has power to pierce the dark; starlight has never shone more brightly for me than since I moved here.

What is wonderful about the light mentioned in this prophecy is that it is not a physical force, nor yet an abstract concept, some kind of philosophical enlightenment. The 'light [that] has dawned' is linked to the birth of a child who will govern on the throne of David (most honoured of Israel's kings), yet will surpass even his rule. We find it hard to read or hear this passage without experiencing it as a direct foretelling of Jesus' birth, but the prophet would simply have been passing on the words and insights as received, without any particular sense of what they might mean. As always, we should remember that biblical prophecy is not 'foretelling' in the sense of predicting the future but rather 'forth-telling', proclaiming truths felt to be divinely inspired. Correct interpretation and application are a different matter, which may well come more easily with hindsight.

---

*Lord Almighty, thank you for the astonishing gift of your Son,*
*Light of the World, Prince of Peace.*

NAOMI STARKEY

# Lightening the load

[Jesus said] 'All things have been committed to me by my Father. No one knows the Son except the Father, and no one knows the Father except the Son and those to whom the Son chooses to reveal him. Come to me, all you who are weary and burdened, and I will give you rest. Take my yoke upon you and learn from me, for I am gentle and humble in heart, and you will find rest for your soul. For my yoke is easy and my burden is light.'

It is always enlightening to look at popular verses in their immediate context. Jesus' gentle and familiar words of welcome to all 'who are weary and burdened' actually follow a powerful declaration of his heaven-bestowed authority. The one who offers welcome is the one with exclusive access to the Father—and the one who has the responsibility to reveal the Father to others. It is the Son of God who declares himself here to be 'gentle and humble in heart', a powerful paradox.

We should note, though, that Jesus does not speak of laying down burdens altogether. He offers 'rest' for the weary but also instruction: 'Take my yoke and learn from me.' We may discover that we are needlessly carrying some burdens through our lives, and that we must give ourselves permission to lay them down—and leave them lying at our Lord's feet. Others, however, may prove to be an unavoidable part of our lives, whether they are burdensome responsibilities, relationships, financial or health circumstances. We may be tempted to despair, yet the Son of God tells us that if we come to him, he will help us. We may not be able to put down our burdens and walk away, but he offers us an 'easy' yoke, one that will make lighter work of the load. This is an invitation to rest for everyone, not just for those who are in a position to take life a little easier.

---

*Lord Jesus, give me wisdom to know which burdens I can leave at your feet and which I should continue to bear as I journey—but grant me the grace of your easy yoke to carry them.*

NAOMI STARKEY

# Answering the call

Shortly before dawn Jesus went out to [the disciples], walking on the lake. When the disciples saw [Jesus] walking on the lake, they were terrified. 'It's a ghost,' they said, and cried out in fear. But Jesus immediately said to them: 'Take courage! It is I. Don't be afraid.' 'Lord, if it's you,' Peter replied, 'tell me to come to you on the water.' 'Come,' he said. Then Peter got down out of the boat, walked on the water and came towards Jesus. But when he saw the wind, he was afraid and, beginning to sink, cried out, 'Lord, save me!' Immediately Jesus reached out his hand and caught him. 'You of little faith,' he said, 'why did you doubt?'

The scene is dramatic: Jesus is on a mountain, praying alone. He has sent the disciples on ahead to cross Lake Galilee, but strong headwinds mean that even the experienced sailors are struggling. We might imagine that Jesus would stay on the mountain, arms raised to heaven, commanding calmer weather. Instead, we have the astonishing events narrated here: he strolls over the water towards his friends, who are, predictably, terrified. Not only that, but he invites Peter to join him. And then, when Peter (quite understandably) falters, Jesus tells him off.

It is as if Jesus is teasing his followers: 'So you want to travel with me? Let's see how trusting you really are. You think I have special powers? Let's see how much you really believe in me.' The challenge is undeniable: he is not only a gentle shepherd, wise teacher and miraculous healer, but one who calls people way beyond their comfort zones, over safe boundaries and literally out on to the deep.

Imagine being adrift in a small boat on a stormy sea, looking desperately for rescue. Then, unbelievably, we see Jesus himself splashing over the wave-tops towards us. We assume that he will climb into the boat and steer us to safety. Instead, he calls to us, above the wind: 'Hey, why not get out of the boat? Come to me!' The invitation is clear… but what is our response?

---

*Lord Jesus, help me to hear your call clearly and then to have the courage to respond.*

NAOMI STARKEY

# Recovering perspective

Then Jesus said to his disciples: 'Therefore I tell you, do not worry about your life, what you will eat; or about your body, what you will wear. For life is more than food, and the body more than clothes. Consider the ravens: they do not sow or reap, they have no storeroom or barn; yet God feeds them. And how much more valuable you are than birds! Who of you by worrying can add a single hour to your life? Since you cannot do this very little thing, why do you worry about the rest?... But seek [your Father's] kingdom, and these things will be given to you as well.'

There are those who take life as it comes, happy to go with the flow and see what turns up. Then there are those who plan and ponder and track possible outcomes from more or less plausible scenarios until they can end up nearly paralysed in case they make the wrong decision. Jesus' words here almost leap off the page with energy, forcing such chronic over-thinkers (and I admit to being one such) to step back, look up, draw breath and regain true perspective.

People sometimes speak of the clarity that comes with crisis, whether it is a distressing personal situation or wider troubles. When floodwaters are rising round your house, you reach instinctively to rescue what you value most. When you know you have only a few months to live, priorities can change dramatically. Jesus is saying here that we can consciously cultivate such clarity. He is not saying that food and drink, clothing and life itself are unimportant. He is saying that these things are gifts from the hands of our Creator God. He is also saying that worrying about these gifts—that hand-wringing, floor-pacing attitude that says, 'Unless I am constantly vigilant, everything will fall apart'—is a monumental waste of time. We are called instead to trust, to be faithful and to let go of unnecessary burdens of angst into the hands of one who cares for us more than we can imagine.

---

*Lord God, teach me trust in place of worry, faith instead of fear, and walk with me into tomorrow.*

NAOMI STARKEY

# Revelling in redemption

But now apart from the law the righteousness of God has been made known, to which the Law and the Prophets testify. This righteousness is given through faith in Jesus Christ to all who believe. There is no difference between Jew and Gentile, for all have sinned and fall short of the glory of God, and all are justified freely by his grace through the redemption that came by Christ Jesus.

During my ordination studies, I spent a term working through Paul's letter to the church in Rome—and I wish I could quote the whole of it here! While selected verses (including those quoted today) are often used to console or challenge us, the letter's magnificent scope and magisterial argument is best appreciated by a read-through from beginning to end, even if it is less than straightforward in places. Today's passage is universal in its scope; it provokes despair, only to turn it at once to breathtaking relief: for 'all' have sinned, 'all' fall short—but, wonderfully, 'all' are redeemed through Christ.

In today's culture, we can shy away from words such as 'sin', fearful of 'putting people off', preferring to speak instead of love, mercy and forgiveness. But when we shut our eyes to our propensity for falling short, and for the idolatrous human habit of denying the true God and putting false gods in his place, our very selves can start to unravel, as our vision narrows to pursuing our own agendas and our ears grow dull to God's call to holiness.

Again and again Paul returns to the same point in his letter, considering it from different angles: the law reveals the hugeness of God's holiness and our corresponding failure to come anywhere near meeting his standards (which are, even so, standards based on his love for us rather than on condemnation). God's priceless gift to us, his children, is his own Son, who died for us so that we might be made right in his Father's eyes.

---

*God our Father, enlarge our hearts to grasp a little more of the immensity of your love revealed in the gift of your redeeming Son, our Saviour Jesus.*

NAOMI STARKEY

# Nurturing love

If I speak in the tongues of men or of angels, but do not have love, I am only a resounding gong or a clanging cymbal. If I have the gift of prophecy and can fathom all mysteries and all knowledge, and if I have a faith that can move mountains, but do not have love, I am nothing. If I give all I possess to the poor and give over my body to hardship that I may boast, but do not have love, I gain nothing... And now these three remain: faith, hope and love. But the greatest of these is love.

Often chosen as a Bible reading for weddings, 1 Corinthians 13 has a far wider application when considered as part of Paul's address to a Greek congregation who were struggling with a number of serious issues and to whom Paul later had to defend his very status as an apostle (2 Corinthians 10—13). He is making the point that however glittering the outward ministry of a church, however socially aware its activities and powerful its preaching, its true effectiveness is measured by the depth and quality of relationships between the individuals who constitute that church.

I recall talking to a friend who was a member of the local 'big church', which drew people from a wide area through the quality of its worship, teaching and children's work. My friend described what she called 'coffee time syndrome'—the habit that too many people had, of striking up conversation with someone, only to catch sight of a more interesting individual over their shoulder and saying a hasty goodbye. The church was excellent in many ways but, for whatever reason, at that time it failed to engender an atmosphere of love and care that would have ensured that every person felt equally valued.

A truly loving fellowship can develop irrespective of musical style, churchmanship, congregation size or physical location. Once it has developed, that love should be prized above all other attributes—and I believe that priority should be non-negotiable for anyone in any kind of leadership role.

---

*Lord Jesus, guide us in developing church fellowships that draw people by the way we love and care for one another.*

NAOMI STARKEY

# Keeping the faith

But you, keep your head in all situations, endure hardship, do the work of an evangelist, discharge all the duties of your ministry. For I am already being poured out like a drink offering, and the time for my departure is near. I have fought the good fight, I have finished the race, I have kept the faith. Now there is in store for me the crown of righteousness, which the Lord, the righteous Judge, will award to me on that day—and not only to me, but also to all who have longed for his appearing.

This passage expresses eloquently and poignantly the sense of a life and ministry drawing to a close. 2 Timothy is grouped as one of three 'pastoral epistles' (along with 1 Timothy and Titus), which Paul wrote to individuals rather than to churches as a whole. The mentor figure (Paul) is offering guidance to his deputy (Timothy), aware that he does not have much time left, even though so much work remains to be done. For Paul, there was no option of continuing; he knew that his life would, before long, be taken from him. Even so, he could say honestly that he had 'kept the faith', remaining true to the Lord who had met him on the way to Damascus and set him on a new road.

More often than not, we have the choice of whether or not to bring a situation to an end—to change jobs, home location or some other aspect of our personal circumstances. Even if we have reached a natural conclusion, it can be hard, even painful, to judge whether or not it is right to finish something, not least because we may feel emotionally tied to the way things currently are. For us, 'keeping the faith' can mean being open to God's summons to move on because, for us, the race is not finished. There is more for us to do in service to our Lord, and we can offer that service in the confidence that, like Paul, whatever sacrifices we make never pass unnoticed by the one who loves us.

---

*Lord Jesus, increase our hope and strengthen our faith*
*so that we too long for your appearing.*

NAOMI STARKEY

# Walking in the light

This is the message we have heard from him and declare to you: God is light; in him there is no darkness at all. If we claim to have fellowship with him and yet walk in the darkness, we lie and do not live out the truth. But if we walk in the light, as he is in the light, we have fellowship with one another, and the blood of Jesus, his Son, purifies us from all sin. If we claim to be without sin, we deceive ourselves and the truth is not in us. If we confess our sins, he is faithful and just and will forgive us our sins and purify us from all unrighteousness.

A month or so after I had settled into my new home, I wondered why I needed to do so much more dusting than in my previous little cottage. Then I looked at the big windows, which let the sunshine pour in as well as offering glimpses of the sea, and I realised the truth: it wasn't a matter of more dust but of more light! There was so much sun that every speck of dust was magnified, every cobweb emphatically highlighted.

Living in the shadows, whether literally or metaphorically, is easier in some respects. It is easier to smooth over difficulties, ignore painful truths and fumble our way round obstacles. Stepping into the light hurts the eyes, forcing us to see and acknowledge the real state of affairs, which may be far messier than we have realised.

As these verses reassure us so profoundly, however, we need not fear coming into God's light. If we are in fellowship with our forgiving, generous Father, we are able to bear the radiance of his presence because we know that whatever dust and dirt is revealed in our lives can be cleansed. Such cleansing then restores our relationships with others so that we can grow together into communities suffused with that same light, shining out for the rest of the world to see.

---

*Give us courage, heavenly Father, to step from darkness into your light and to continue to walk in that light with you, day by day.*

NAOMI STARKEY

# The letter to the Hebrews

Ever since I began studying theology I have felt that the letter to the Hebrews is one of the most impressive documents in the New Testament. It has a carefully constructed style and a high-quality use of the Greek language and is consciously Christological. It offers deep and valuable insights that have shaped the subsequent development of the Christian tradition. However, it also presents us with questions. Unlike almost all the other letters in the New Testament, it gives us no information about the identity of the author, the locality in which it was written or the circumstances of the recipients.

As I reflect on the various arguments about 'who, what and where' in relation to this letter, I'm left thinking that it was probably written to a group of Jewish Christians, possibly living in Rome, who were struggling with their newfound faith as well as living under increasing opposition and even persecution. The author is deeply concerned about the possibility that they might abandon the faith altogether. It was clearly written before AD95 because it is quoted by Clement of Rome at about that time, and possibly even before AD70, as it makes no reference to the fall of the temple. The letter is full of urgent appeals, earnest requests, admonitions and sometimes even threats.

I will be focusing my reflections on chapters 4—7, the part of the letter that is devoted to portraying the superiority of Jesus' priesthood over the kind of priesthood that had been hitherto experienced in Judaism. It is a section of the letter that reaches a climax in the author's high view of Christology. What I find particularly interesting is the way in which the author uses the 'memory' of the past to change the present. The author urges readers to recollect their history in order to understand the superiority and divinity of Christ, and so to remain faithful. Readers are presented with examples of witnesses to a model faith, from Abel to Moses. Clearly the author is rooted in and competent to explore the rudiments of Jewish theology and offers readers a kind of 'refresher course' by reminding them of some quintessential origins—Christ's and their own.

ANDREW JONES

# Place of rest

Therefore, while the promise of entering his rest is still open, let us take care that none of you should seem to have failed to reach it. For indeed the good news came to us just as to them; but the message they heard did not benefit them, because they were not united by faith with those who listened.

The situation in some local churches at the time when this letter was written was lax, and the author aims to combat that laxity by offering these believers a refresher course, to remind them of the 'story' that they were dangerously close to forgetting. Even two or three generations on, some Christians had become blasé about certain truths—that Christ was the basis of the freedom from law and sin; that the death of Jesus freed them from servitude; that the sacrifice of Christ blotted out human sin, all of which established a new and better covenant between God and human beings.

These verses at the beginning of Hebrews 4 continue the author's exposition of Psalm 95. The first part (3:12–19) hit a note of warning against the loss of faith and suggested that the Christians were grumbling as the people of old grumbled against Moses and Aaron (Numbers 14:2–4). Here in the second part (4:1–11), the author applies scripture in a practical way to the readers' situation, suggesting that faithfulness will enable them to enter the rest that God took on the seventh day of creation (Genesis 2:2). Here we see a movement from warning to promise—from ticking off the people for falling away from God to reminding them of the opportunity that God offers to enter his own place of rest.

The author comes close to rewriting the last verse of Psalm 95 ('Therefore in my anger I swore, "They shall not enter my rest".') The original is an angry line, but now it becomes a promise to those who are bordering on faithlessness and failure to believe the good news that they have heard from God. It is an invitation to be in his presence and his rest.

---

*May we accept that invitation today and rejoice in God's presence and rest.*

ANDREW JONES

# One with us

For we do not have a high priest who is unable to sympathise with our weaknesses, but we have one who in every respect has been tested as we are, yet without sin. Let us therefore approach the throne of grace with boldness, so that we may receive mercy and find grace to help in time of need.

Today again we see the transition from a God who warns (4:11–13) to a God who promises (vv. 14–16). This promise comes in the context of the dominant theme in my selections from the letter—the superiority of Jesus' priesthood. In today's verses the author is not contrasting Jesus with other 'lower' priests. These verses are better understood positively, as a description of the way in which his readers should regard the priesthood of Christ as a great gift.

In verse 15, the gift is that of Christ's sympathy: people don't deal with testing times alone. This 'sympathy' does not mean that he feels pity, compassion and sorrowfulness for their troubles. Rather, Christ is able to sympathise because, through a significant common experience, he has stood in that place of weakness and total vulnerability—the only difference being that Jesus never succumbed to weakness. By virtue of this, Christ's followers are able to rejoice because the barriers between God and people have been removed. All people, not just priests, are now invited to approach God.

Verse 16 takes the gift even further. The invitation to approach the throne is not meant to be understood in the sense of approaching through worship. The throne of grace is where God sits and from which he is able to 'promise' more than 'judge'. This is the place from which God offers the abundant gifts of mercy and grace in time of need. Although this is God's throne and not Jesus' throne, the dominant note here is that our confident access to God has been assured by the redemptive work of Jesus.

---

*Sometimes we all need help. The 'help' mentioned in verse 16 is to be understood directly as God's response to his people's troubles. What a tremendous gift to be appreciated today!*

ANDREW JONES

# Learning obedience through suffering

In the days of his flesh, Jesus offered up prayers and supplications... to the one who was able to save him from death... Although he was a Son, he learned obedience through what he suffered; and having been made perfect, he became the source of eternal salvation for all who obey him, having been designated by God a high priest according to the order of Melchizedek.

Over the years I have often encountered people's interest in the idea of Jesus as a Son and their dilemmas as they try to make sense of the image. Questions are constantly asked about the meaning of the word 'Son'. People want to know what differentiates Son of God from Son of Man, Son of David and so on. In our reading today, the word comes up again, but with no indication of whose Son Jesus is.

It has been suggested that these verses are an ancient hymn, similar to Philippians 2:6–11. The hymn reflects on Jesus as a Son in two ways: on the one hand, he became Son when he was exalted and, on the other hand, he always was Son because he existed with the Father before he ever appeared on earth (John 1:1–2, 18). Both ways of speaking about Jesus as Son are valid, but my impression is that the author of these verses is speaking of the Son not as eternally divine but as fully and completely incarnate as a human being. The Son, it appears, learnt full obedience in the only way possible in an incarnate human life, through submission to the will of God under the pressure of emotional shock and physical distress.

Further, this is the sense in which the Son can properly be described as 'perfect'. The author regards the perfect obedience of Christ in his sufferings as the reason why he became the source of eternal salvation—'eternal' in the sense that it relates to the world to come. It is interesting that, in verse 7, the author mentions Jesus' prayer that his sufferings might be removed. Christ prayed to be saved from death, yet by his death obtained the salvation of all. Having learnt to obey, he saves those who obey.

---

*We pray knowing that prayers may be answered in ways we don't expect.*

ANDREW JONES

# Growing in faith

For everyone who lives on milk, being still an infant, is unskilled in the word of righteousness. But solid food is for the mature, for those whose faculties have been trained by practice to distinguish good from evil.

Today we reach some verses from the central section of the letter to the Hebrews (5:11—6:20). The section begins with a long exhortation to spiritual renewal, but it also contains a stern rebuke. The author finds it difficult to speak plainly about Jesus' priesthood because his readers have become complacent, almost faithless, and forgetful of the Christian story. This central section contains the fullest presentation of the letter's distinctive teaching about Christ's high priesthood and his sacrifice, but the author hesitates because he doubts their ability to appreciate this teaching. Too many of them are like infants, unable to appreciate the deeper aspects of the Christian faith; but still, he ends up offering a clearly articulated and theologically competent teaching of Christ's superior priesthood.

If we read the letter further, it appears that, on the whole, the author doesn't believe that his readers, when push comes to shove, will abandon the faith, and the very fact that he has written in this way goes to show that he has a deep and pastoral concern for them.

Memory plays a vital role throughout biblical history. Indeed, it could be said that memory has played and continues to play an essential role in all religious traditions. As the different religions meet, scriptures are read, ceremonies are performed and actions happen, in order to worship but also to remember the 'story'. Much of the Old Testament centres on God's people recollecting events from the past that nourish the life of faith—events in which God became a reality. Moses spent much of his time encouraging the Israelites in the wilderness to remember their experience of God and to pass it on, and the same can be said about the prophets.

---

*Today's church has the task of equipping people to grow in the faith and to be confident in passing on the deeper things—the solid food of faith.*

ANDREW JONES

# Basics of truth

Let us go on towards perfection, leaving behind the basic teaching about Christ, and not laying again the foundation: repentance from dead works and faith towards God, instruction about baptisms, laying on of hands, resurrection of the dead, and eternal judgement. And we will do this, if God permits.

The author has already declared that his readers have failed in their duty to develop adequately their understanding of Christian teaching and that they need to be refreshed in the basics. Strangely, though, rather than providing a refresher course, he goes on to present them with pretty deep stuff! This might appear paradoxical, but the author believes that it is, in fact, the deep challenges of faith that will ultimately move his readers on. He has rebuked them for spiritual lethargy and now he turns to six important faith matters—possibly in the hope that they will 'buck up' spiritually. These six elements may originally have been part of an ancient manual of teachings.

This list may offer us clues to what the emerging non-Pauline churches thought were essential points of Christian instruction—particularly the churches that maintained strong Jewish links. Indeed, it may well be that the list of six faith matters, which is not exhaustive and is not mentioned in the same way again, formed part of the author's own pre-baptismal preparation and his own personal experience of Christian teaching.

However, it is an interesting list from a contemporary point of view as well. Repentance and faith are our own twofold response to God's word and God's presence in our lives. Baptism lies at the heart of our Christian lives and continues to be our sacrament, or mark of covenant, both with God and each other. Hands continue to be used in blessings, healings, initiation and prayer. We are who we are because of the resurrection of Christ, and we will one day be with him in glory and judgement.

---

*Let's thank God for an opportunity of rejoicing, for we have been blessed in our lives of faith by these six fundamentals.*

ANDREW JONES

# Keep working and loving

Even though we speak in this way, beloved, we are confident of better things in your case, things that belong to salvation. For God is not unjust; he will not overlook your work and the love that you showed for his sake in serving the saints, as you still do. And we want each one of you to show the same diligence, so as to realise the full assurance of hope to the very end.

The author's mood seems to be changing: instead of earnestness, we now encounter mildness. In verse 9, for the first and last time, he addresses his readers as 'beloved'; indeed, this is the only occasion in the whole of the letter when he shows any warmth towards them. But this does not mean that he has forgotten the danger that they may fall away from the Christian faith. On the contrary, the mood change is linked to the fact that the danger is still very real; by being mild, the author is trying a different approach. Behind it lies his conviction that, despite their spiritual lethargy, there is still hope that his readers may not give up completely.

Today's verses give us a clue concerning his reason for that hope, which is their love towards fellow Christians. Further evidence is mentioned later in the letter (10:33b–34a), and the author is convinced that such behaviour manifests a love towards God, hence his use of the description 'the saints'. Their zeal in helping and loving one another should be matched by their zeal in persevering as Christians.

Our selection today ends on a familiar note. It is generally clear in the letter that the readers were initially enthusiastic and eager in their Christian faith, and in many ways that was natural. But they have become 'sluggish', showing signs, despite mutual service and love, of wavering. In many ways, again, that was typical. However, the author's conviction is that only by continuing to be enthusiastic and eager will they yield the fruits of their faithfulness.

---

*O Lord, in my own life as a Christian, may I be strengthened and inspired to be eager in my service to others and in my faithfulness to you. Amen*

ANDREW JONES

# Anchor of faith

We have this hope, a sure and steadfast anchor of the soul, a hope that enters the inner shrine behind the curtain, where Jesus, a forerunner on our behalf, has entered, having become a high priest for ever according to the order of Melchizedek.

Talk of Christian hope runs right through this letter, and here the author uses the image of an anchor that extends into what he calls the 'inner shrine'. With this image, he is seeking to convey a conviction that the anchor of hope guarantees inner peace and security in life.

The inner shrine behind the curtain is an allusion to the tabernacle of Moses in the wilderness (Exodus 26:31–33), which was an earthly picture of the heavenly home of God. The tabernacle of Moses had a curtain through which access was gained to the Holy of Holies, and is used here as a metaphor for the curtain through which Christ gained entry into heaven. As the author's train of thought continues to develop in the letter, this metaphor becomes central to the way in which he seeks to convey the high priesthood of Christ. Jesus' entry through the heavenly curtain and into the shrine brings his atoning sacrifice to its climax.

The hope that runs right through this letter relates to the redemption that Christ achieved for God's children. Christ entered the eternal shrine, beyond the curtain, as our forerunner (v. 20). God's children can be hopeful because Christ is already there, and his presence is a powerful witness of our hope. Interestingly, the image of Christ as forerunner echoes Christ's own words about going to heaven to prepare a place for his disciples (John 14:2–3). However, here in the letter to the Hebrews, his disappearance beyond the curtain and his entry into the inner shrine mean more than simply a 'preparation' for others. They are a proclamation of a divine ministry accomplished—a redemption—and they announce the first fruits of a hopeful glory for his followers.

---

*May our anchors sustain us in the storms of life.*

ANDREW JONES

# King of righteousness, king of peace

This 'King Melchizedek of Salem, priest of the Most High God, met Abraham as he was returning from defeating the kings and blessed him'; and to him Abraham apportioned 'one-tenth of everything'. His name, in the first place, means 'king of righteousness'; next he is also king of Salem, that is, 'king of peace'.

We have already encountered the name Melchizedek (literally 'king of righteousness') in previous readings. He was probably an 18th-century BC king of Salem, a place-name that refers to Jerusalem in Psalm 76:2 and in some 14th-century BC tablets (from Tel el-Amarna), when Jerusalem is named as 'Uru-salim'. In Psalm 110:4, Melchizedek is a symbol of an ideal priest-king.

The Old Testament context for the reference to Melchizedek is Genesis 14:18–20; the author intends to argue for the superiority of Jesus' priesthood over even the most perfect Old Testament priest. The reflection develops quite carefully through Hebrews 7, seeking to demonstrate four essentials: basic information about Melchizedek (vv. 1–3), his superiority over Abraham and Levi (vv. 4–10), Jesus as a replacement for the levitical priesthood (vv. 11–19) and the ultimate superiority and perfection of Jesus' priesthood (vv. 20–28).

From the Old Testament references, Melchizedek was clearly a significant person: he blessed Abraham, his priesthood was accompanied by God's oath, and any priesthood according to 'the order of Melchizedek' is considered to be eternal. If Jesus is superior to him, there is no longer a need for numerous (levitical) priests who are replaced after death, because Jesus continues for ever and offers all the intercession that is needed. The sacrifice of the cross is once and for all. However, Melchizedek is both a name and a title. He is called, first, the king of righteousness and, second, the king of peace. We encounter here something highly appropriate: an insistence that the name and the title belong together and in the order given. Peace with God is firmly established on the righteousness of God.

---

*Let us pray for the peace of Jerusalem and for the reconciliation of her people.*

ANDREW JONES

# New priesthood

Now if perfection had been attainable through the levitical priesthood—for the people received the law under this priesthood—what further need would there have been to speak of another priest arising according to the order of Melchizedek, rather than one according to the order of Aaron? For when there is a change in the priesthood, there is necessarily a change in the law as well.

Attention now moves away from Melchizedek and Abraham to the priests of the Levi tradition and, later, to the high priesthood of Jesus (7:20–28). There is an interesting balance in this chapter between the author's negativity towards the priests of Levi and his positivity towards the priesthood of Jesus. His basic argument is that the law of Moses is ineffective in enabling full access to God, and he insists on the importance of the eternal priesthood of Christ, which provides perfect access to God.

These verses are about gaining the access to God that Jesus has achieved. The author is concerned that the sluggishness of his readers towards faith is dangerous: it will be a block to true access. In the Jewish tradition, the law was given to Israel as a means of obtaining that access and of establishing a relationship with God. Consequently, the levitical priesthood was the instrument by which the law was made able to achieve its purpose. For me, the principle expressed in verse 11 is foundational to the argument that runs through the entire letter to the Hebrews. The author is saying that the failure of the levitical priesthood to provide lasting access to and union with God means that there is an urgent need for a different kind of priesthood.

We can compare what the author is saying in these two verses with what Paul says elsewhere. For Paul, as for the author of Hebrews, the law is temporary (Galatians 3:24). Its purpose is to raise awareness of sin; it does not provide access to God's justification. Thus, the law belongs to a period of preparation, which must now give way, through the cross, to a period of fulfilment.

---

*Lord, thank you for periods of preparation and fulfilment in our own lives.*

ANDREW JONES

# Priesthood revealed in Christ

Now the one of whom these things are spoken belonged to another tribe, from which no one has ever served at the altar. For it is evident that our Lord was descended from Judah, and in connection with that tribe Moses said nothing about priests.

The author of the letter to the Hebrews is both challenging and radical. If I had been one of those sluggish hearers, I would have found his teaching desperately challenging. Could he be right? How dare he be so arrogant! Do I not have the right to decide for myself? On the other hand, had I been someone on the religious margins, not knowing which way to turn, it could have sounded excitingly radical. There must have been many hearers who had fallen short of the law of Moses, encountering the wrath and judgement of those levitical priests. All of a sudden, here is a preacher telling them that both the law and the priesthood should be given a radical shake-up, so that something different, fresh and exhilarating could emerge before their very eyes.

First-generation Christians knew that Jesus was descended from King David, of the tribe of Judah (Romans 1:3; Matthew 1:1–6), a tribe that attracted hopes for liberation but was not connected with priesthood. So the author is saying that the levitical priesthood has been replaced not by another tribal priesthood but by something utterly new and radical.

Again, verses 13 and 14 balance (strategically, maybe) negativity and positivity. First the author says that no one from the tribe of Judah has ever been allowed to perform religious ceremonies at the altar. Then he goes on to say that, by virtue of this change of priesthood, it has actually happened.

---

*I wonder whether I would have found this teaching challenging or radical—possibly a bit of both. But one thing is for certain, it is the radical part that would have sent me home skipping! At last Israel had the chance to trust a priesthood that had its power in heaven—in the eternal realm, not controlled by men and women.*

ANDREW JONES

# Hope leads us to God

There is, on the one hand, the abrogation of an earlier commandment because it was weak and ineffectual (for the law made nothing perfect); there is, on the other hand, the introduction of a better hope, through which we approach God.

Here we have more negatives and positives. Negatively, the law had to be replaced because it was weak, ineffectual and unable to offer life in all its abundance. The author probably believed that the law, and certainly those who controlled it, were too intimately bound to worldly affairs. The author seems to be saying that the system was being held up by law and not by love, without which nothing is good (1 Corinthians 13:3). Even more, maybe the law did express God's will but it also prevented full access for those needing God's grace and love. The author is not condemning the law but he is stating that it cannot be enough; by it, union with God remains superficial. But there is a positive note: the law was changed because a more authentic hope was revealed.

Hope lies at the heart of the Christian proclamation, but it is not the same as the Jewish hope for a better world—the hope that the world might come to realise God's eternal destiny for all his people. The new idea that the author of this letter announced (as did the other apostles) was that the Christian hope is not fixed for ever and static—simply there to dictate lifestyle. Christian hope looks beyond death and to people's ultimate goal of union with God. According to the law, only priests could gain full access to God (Exodus 19:22). Now, with this new hope, all people have access to that gift and all can share in the priesthood (1 Peter 2:5).

---

*The new announcement of hope meant that something which was an impossible dream for many people could become a reality through the gift of sharing in Christ's priesthood. This letter is telling us today that the same gift can be ours.*

ANDREW JONES

# Christ the interceding one

Consequently he is able for all time to save those who approach God through him, since he always lives to make intercession for them.

In the final section of chapter 7, the author bids farewell to Melchizedek and the focus moves to Jesus. The challenge in this section is the question, what exactly is Christ's priesthood? Verses 25–27 offer us a clue.

Today, in verse 25, we see that his priesthood is one of intercession, praying constantly to the Father for us. Tomorrow we will discover that, by virtue of his exaltation, he is the mediator between us and God, and on Saturday we will encounter the implications of his ultimate self-sacrifice.

Verse 25 suggests that the purpose of Christ's priestly ministry is the salvation of those who come to God through him. Salvation here refers to the achievement of ultimate access to God through a relationship with Christ.

The idea of Christ as intercessor is not peculiar to this letter. In his letter to the Romans, Paul announces with great gusto that Christ sits at God's right hand to intercede for us (Romans 8:33–34). I think, too, that Paul and the author of Hebrews are echoing one of the great 'servant songs' in Isaiah, where the exalted servant is interceding for the transgressors (Isaiah 53:12). Christ showed himself as the one who prayed for others during his earthly ministry. He prayed for Peter at the last supper (Luke 22:32) and his so-called high-priestly prayer at the end of the supper was for others (John 17). In his prayers, Jesus made intercession for all who would come to God through him. And, as the exalted Christ in heaven, he continues the same ministry of prayer, but now at God's right hand.

Let us not think of that in simple human terms. He is not at his Father's right-hand side, standing upright in a prayerful position. To be at God's right hand means that, as the exalted one, he can intercede in the full confidence that God will hear.

---

*Jesus, please pray for us today.*

ANDREW JONES

# Christ the exalted one

For it was fitting that we should have such a high priest, holy, blameless, undefiled, separated from sinners, and exalted above the heavens.

As the exalted one, Jesus is able to mediate between us human beings and God. Such mediation was essential in order to prepare access to God's eternal presence. The opening of verse 26 seeks to show that, during his earthly life, Jesus was humanly perfect as well as being perfectly human. The list of virtues serves to contrast his human perfection with the ceremonial requirements of the priests of Levi. They were required to be 'holy' (set apart) to conduct the liturgical parts of worship; they were 'blameless' because they had been ritually cleansed of their sins; they were 'undefiled' because they stuck to the rules that told them how to avoid situations of defilement; they were 'separated from sinners' through their obedience to the law.

By contrast, Jesus was 'holy' by virtue of his Sonship and his participation in the life of God himself; he was 'blameless' because his divine origin prevented him from being capable of hurt, offence and malice; he was 'undefiled' because his spirit was pure and without stain; he was 'separated from sinners' because he had entered into the very place where sin is absent and sat down at the right hand of the Father in glory.

The picture of the new priesthood that the author seeks to paint (and chapter 7 sees him in full flow) contains all of these characteristics. In essence, though, what makes the new priesthood unique is simply that it is Jesus. The author is not providing an ideal job description for any priest; rather, he is painting a picture of the exalted Christ fully at work. The implicit radical reminder of the author's announcement is that, though now exalted, Christ was also tempted on earth, cried desperately to God for help, and suffered.

---

*It comforts me that, from his exalted place in glory, it is quite possible to envisage Christ remembering his own human sufferings even as we cry out to him in the depths of our own sufferings.*

ANDREW JONES

# Christ's self-offering

Unlike the other high priests, he has no need to offer sacrifices day after day, first for his own sins, and then for those of the people; this he did once for all when he offered himself.

The law of Moses does not mention any instruction prescribing that levitical priests should perform the sacrificial rites on a daily basis, either for their own spiritual well-being or for the salvation of the people. The levitical priests may well have felt the need to offer up sin-offerings on a daily basis but in reality they did not do so. It is probable that the author knew this, but the reason for the slight contradiction is perhaps to be found in Leviticus 6:22, where the high priest, on his anointing, offers the sacrifice 'perpetually'. Again, in essence, the author is seeking to contrast the inadequacy of levitical sacrifice with the full adequacy of the sacrifice of Jesus. Contrasted with the 'daily' or 'perpetual' sacrifices of the high priest, Jesus offered himself only once.

Interestingly, this is the first time the author has mentioned Jesus as an offering or a sacrifice, and it is a self-offering for the people, not for himself. Elsewhere in the New Testament there are references to the death of Jesus as a voluntary offering: he said that he had come 'to give his life a ransom for many' (Mark 10:45), and he spoke of his blood being poured out 'for many' (Mark 14:24). Indeed, on the cross there were no words of protest but rather a willing self-offering to God on behalf of the people.

---

*In our various ministries we can learn from these marks of Jesus' high priesthood. He prays for us, so let us pray for each other. He mediates on our behalf, so let us mediate reconciliation in the world and between each other. He offered a self-sacrifice for humanity, so let us be self-sacrificial in our dealings with one another.*

ANDREW JONES

# Exodus 2—15 in the light of Christ

When we read the Bible, we let the whole Bible interpret the whole Bible. Better still, we read the Bible in the light of the worship and faith of the church through the ages, or the light of Christ. In the following notes on Exodus 2—15, we will look at the early life of Moses in this perspective, as a reminder of the bonds between the Old and New Testaments.

No figure is more essential to Judaism, Christianity and Islam than Moses. He was seen historically (though not by most contemporary scholars) as the author of the first five books of the Old Testament, so Paul writes, about the Jews' blindness to Jesus, that 'whenever Moses is read, a veil lies over their minds; but when one turns to the Lord, the veil is removed' (2 Corinthians 3:15–16).

So, we will follow the origin, flight and call of Moses, his receipt of miraculous powers, his confrontations with Pharaoh and complaints to God, his part in bringing disaster on Egypt and his leadership of the Jewish exodus through the Red Sea.

Many of these scenes are part of Christian liturgy—for example, in the Easter season, when the deliverance of Israel from slavery is read as a prophecy of the deliverance of God's new people, the Church, from bondage to sin and death by the resurrection of Jesus. In this way, Old and New Testaments come together in our worship.

The obvious parallels between the life and work of Moses and of Jesus are helpful reminders of the unity of the Bible. The stories illuminate one another and bring out the wonder of the God who, far from being aloof, shows himself down-to-earth in history, with a bias towards the underprivileged. Exodus 2—15 is a demonstration of suffering yet triumphant faith, concluding with the deliverance song of Moses: 'I will sing to the Lord, for he has triumphed gloriously... The Lord is my strength and my might, and he has become my salvation' (15:1–2).

JOHN TWISLETON

# The origin of Moses

The daughter of Pharaoh came down to bathe at the river, while her attendants walked beside the river. She saw the basket among the reeds and sent her maid to bring it. When she opened it, she saw the child. He was crying, and she took pity on him. 'This must be one of the Hebrews' children,' she said... Pharaoh's daughter said to [the child's mother], 'Take this child and nurse it for me, and I will give you your wages.' So the woman took the child and nursed it. When the child grew up, she brought him to Pharaoh's daughter, and she took him as her son. She named him Moses, 'because', she said, 'I drew him out of the water.'

The extraordinary parallels between the lives of Moses and Jesus help us make sense of our two-volume Bible. They are the lead figures of Old and New Testaments respectively, with the latter illuminating the former and the former opening up facets of Christ to us. Since our 'life is hidden with Christ in God' (Colossians 3:3), reflecting upon Moses is bound to have implications for us.

The births of Moses and Jesus are remarkable in the way they both enter scenarios of conflict and wrong-foot their adversaries. Moses moves from abandonment on the river to adoption by the highest earthly power of his day. God in Christ hides himself at Bethlehem and is overcome by evil powers upon the cross so that he can triumph over death and reveal to us the resurrection.

As we live in Jesus Christ, we too will be subversive in holding the eternal perspective of him 'who abolished death and brought life and immortality to light through the gospel' (2 Timothy 1:10). By faith we are able to reach beyond the rush of time to things that will never pass away. As Moses' birth brought new beginnings to God's people, so it was with Jesus—but what he began will never end and possesses unalterable newness.

---

*God 'has rescued us from the power of darkness and transferred us into the kingdom of his beloved Son, in whom we have redemption, the forgiveness of sins' (Colossians 1:13–14).*

JOHN TWISLETON

# The flight of Moses

One day, after Moses had grown up, he went out to his people and saw their forced labour. He saw an Egyptian beating a Hebrew, one of his kinsfolk. He looked this way and that, and seeing no one he killed the Egyptian and hid him in the sand. When he went out the next day, he saw two Hebrews fighting; and he said to the one who was in the wrong, 'Why do you strike your fellow Hebrew?' He answered, 'Who made you a ruler and judge over us? Do you mean to kill me as you killed the Egyptian?' Then Moses was afraid and thought, 'Surely the thing is known.' When Pharaoh heard of it, he sought to kill Moses. But Moses fled from Pharaoh. He settled in the land of Midian.

Our picture of Moses draws on the biblical record alone. Historical research shows the plausibility of that record, in which a group of Hebrew workers escape Egypt and head via Sinai to Palestine. In this incident we see Moses, Egyptian-named, first entering his role as mediator between the power of Egypt and his underprivileged kinsfolk. We see Christ, universal mediator between humanity and God, prefigured in the local and sinful mediation of Moses.

In consequence of the killing, Moses is exiled to the territory of the nomadic Midianites, where he takes a Gentile bride (another pointer to Jesus Christ, who has taken us as his bride, the Church: Ephesians 5:25). This exile is spiritually formative for Moses, who returns, like Jesus, after 'hidden years', to free his kinsfolk more profoundly through a divine commission.

In today's passage we see a pointer to our redemption—how the immensity of God's love, shown to us in the mediation and shed blood of Jesus, covers our death-dealing sinfulness. Biblical heroes such as Moses, David and Paul all had blood on their hands, but this was no obstacle to their being taken on by God. How can we doubt his readiness to welcome and take us on?

---

*O God, we thank you for sending Jesus as mediator and for the way he opens up the scripture to us, so that we are drawn closer to you. Amen*

JOHN TWISLETON

# The call of Moses

Moses was keeping the flock of his father-in-law Jethro, the priest of Midian; he led his flock beyond the wilderness, and came to Horeb, the mountain of God. There the angel of the Lord appeared to him in a flame of fire out of a bush; he looked, and the bush was blazing, yet it was not consumed. Then Moses said, 'I must turn aside and look at this great sight, and see why the bush is not burned up.' When the Lord saw that he had turned aside to see, God called to him out of the bush, 'Moses, Moses!' And he said, 'Here I am.'

Moses was a miracle man by any reckoning, as founder of three religions. Without him, there would be no Old Testament, New Testament or Islam. Whatever historians make of him (his existence is pretty well undisputed), the story of his miraculous call by God resonates with everything we read about this leader who alone makes intelligible the galvanising of Judaism, its sequel in the new Moses (Jesus Christ) and the dynamic of the Church.

My own calling to the priesthood came as God spoke silently to my heart of his future for me, through a leaf on a tree after a time of retreat, so I identify profoundly with this passage. Is there a natural explanation for the 'burning bush', such as the sun shining on red berries or the kindling of natural gas? However the bush was lit, it ignited Moses' heart. Through him, a people were gathered to God who would eventually return to Horeb (or Sinai) to experience God's holy fire (Exodus 19:18).

The God and Father of Jesus is a God who reveals himself. That revelation is by the Holy Spirit, who spoke through the prophets (starting with Moses), made God's Word flesh in Jesus, and speaks to us still, leading us 'into all the truth' (John 16:13). Christianity is in no way made up—no one could make it up—but the unalterable newness of Jesus is made real to us generation after generation, individual by individual.

---

*Speak, Lord, for your servant is listening. You have the words of eternal life (1 Samuel 3:9; John 6:68).*

JOHN TWISLETON

# Moses given miraculous powers

Then Moses answered, 'But suppose they do not believe me or listen to me, but say, "The Lord did not appear to you."' The Lord said to him, 'What is that in your hand?' He said, 'A staff.' And he said, 'Throw it on the ground.' So he threw the staff on the ground, and it became a snake; and Moses drew back from it. Then the Lord said to Moses, 'Reach out your hand, and seize it by the tail'—so he reached out his hand and grasped it, and it became a staff in his hand—'so that they may believe that the Lord, the God of their ancestors, the God of Abraham, the God of Isaac, and the God of Jacob, has appeared to you.'

Like the ministry of Jesus, the ministry of Moses was accredited from above. Both holy men drew attention to their teaching, and the God they were teaching about, by supernatural means—in this case, Moses' scary staff. Miracles are windows into reality, since God is more real than this ephemeral world, and the eye of faith sees that this is true. Miracles never compel faith (as we see in Pharaoh's response to Moses), but they regularly awaken people to God.

As we compare the miracles of Moses and Jesus, we can see an ethical evolution happening: Moses' miracles are spectacular rather than ethical, while Jesus' are more geared to releasing individuals from sin, sickness and bondage, and bringing them into right-minded humanity. This evolution connects with the 1000 years or so between the two, and also with our own perception of the miraculous, which is influenced by the expansion of scientific knowledge over the last 500 years.

As we reflect on the exodus story as the chronicle of God's greatest act of power in history prior to the resurrection of Jesus, we are invited to consider how much our own way forward in life is guided by the God who creates everything out of nothing, delivers Israel out of Egypt and brings life out of death.

---

*Lord God of power and might, work your wonders among us so that others, seeing your power and might, come to bow down before you in the company of believers. Amen*

JOHN TWISLETON

# Moses and Aaron before Pharaoh

Moses and Aaron went to Pharaoh and said, 'Thus says the Lord, the God of Israel, "Let my people go, so that they may celebrate a festival to me in the wilderness."' But Pharaoh said, 'Who is the Lord, that I should heed him and let Israel go? I do not know the Lord, and I will not let Israel go.' Then they said, 'The God of the Hebrews has revealed himself to us; let us go a three days' journey into the wilderness to sacrifice to the Lord our God, or he will fall upon us with pestilence or sword.' But the king of Egypt said to them, 'Moses and Aaron, why are you taking the people away from their work? Get to your labours!'

The story of Moses moves up a gear as he finally presents himself with Aaron to Pharaoh. Such access would have varied, depending on the incumbent Pharaoh, but, since Moses had been brought up in Pharaoh's harem, he would have been extra privileged.

Granted access, and with the mandate of God and his fellow Hebrews, Moses presents here a more modest petition than he will ultimately make and be granted in the exodus. Asking permission to go and sacrifice to the Lord in the wilderness shows respect for the Egyptian ban on Hebrew religious practice and serves to test the waters with Pharaoh.

'I do not know the Lord, and I will not let Israel go,' is Pharaoh's implacable response. The king of Egypt's ignorance of God is demonstrated by his injustice, manifested further in the imposition of a heavier regime on the Israelites, removing free straw from the brick works (5:7–8). When God makes himself known to Pharaoh, it will be, on that account, through an experience of his wrath.

On the cross, Christians see what sin looks like to God, as Jesus bears for us its affront to God's holiness. This is prefigured in the affront that Moses and his fellows bore, of Pharaoh's unjust dealings—something that godly people can experience in any age.

---

*Consider the things you are impatient about. Ask God to help you revise your judgement so that you retain only his impatience with wrongs that need righting.*

JOHN TWISLETON

# Moses complains to God

Moses turned again to the Lord and said, 'O Lord, why have you mistreated this people? Why did you ever send me? Since I first came to Pharaoh to speak in your name, he has mistreated this people, and you have done nothing at all to deliver your people.' Then the Lord said to Moses, 'Now you shall see what I will do to Pharaoh: indeed, by a mighty hand he will let them go; by a mighty hand he will drive them out of his land.'

All prayer is answered, whether by a green ('yes'), red ('no') or amber ('wait and see') light from heaven. Knowing our Bible assists our prayer by filling out both our knowledge of God and of our deepest and most immediate needs, so that we pray aright. Just as many of the Collects in the Anglican prayer book start by invoking a quality of God (such as mercy) and go on to request a gift that is related to it (for example, forgiveness), Moses' complaint about injustice presumes God to be just, loving and all-knowing.

Complaining to God is a very biblical kind of prayer. We see it, for example, in Psalm 44:23: 'Rouse yourself! Why do you sleep, O Lord? Awake, do not cast us off for ever!' This robust engagement with God in prayer is encouraged by Jesus in his story of the persistent widow who complains successfully to a judge (Luke 18:1–8). The engagement of Jesus with the needy in his earthly life was coupled with his own frequent prayer times, which are occasionally opened to us to show his deep, passionate love.

'By a mighty hand he will let them go,' says the Lord (6:1). This amber light in answer to Moses' prayer speaks of a might beyond that of Pharaoh, his wizards and his soldiers. God is ruling and overruling through a heaven-sent chance to free his people from slavery, showing that 'human wrath serves only to praise him' (Psalm 76:10).

---

*Jesus gave us the Lord's Prayer so that we might echo his desire for the establishment of God's rule in the world. Join his complaint against evil by slowly saying the Lord's Prayer in your heart after hearing today's news summary.*

JOHN TWISLETON

# Moses and the disasters for Egypt

[Moses] lifted up the staff and struck the water in the river, and all the water in the river was turned into blood, and the fish in the river died. The river stank so that the Egyptians could not drink its water, and there was blood throughout the whole land of Egypt. But the magicians of Egypt did the same by their secret arts; so Pharaoh's heart remained hardened, and he would not listen to them, as the Lord had said.

Moses and Jesus head up the Old and New Testaments. Both were born as Hebrews, hid in Egypt as children, performed miracles and interceded before God for the needy. Jesus turned water into wine (John 2:1–11). Here, Moses turns water into blood—a sign of what is coming in the last of the disasters that God brings to Egypt, the death of the firstborn, which in turn is a pointer to Christ.

The Bible is literally a library (Greek *biblia*) containing books and writings that are enormously varied: poetry, prose, law, legend, hymnody and historical record. Scripture is God's word to us through this variety of human writing. Since that word shines in the face of Jesus Christ, we look back at the story of Moses knowing that he 'was faithful in all God's house as a servant, to testify to the things that would be spoken later' (Hebrews 3:5).

As we look at the record of Moses (or, indeed, the Old Testament as a whole) in the light of Christ, some of that record is lit up, while other texts are darkened. We rejoice in the exodus, the sign of redemption, but we are troubled by the record of disasters seemingly willed by God. The fact that Christians can read Moses through Christ is evidence of how God, who 'long ago… spoke to our ancestors in many and varied ways by the prophets… has spoken to us by a Son' who is 'the exact imprint of God's very being' (Hebrews 1:1–3). Our knowledge that God is Christ-like helps us to sift Old Testament pictures of God for their saving truth, in which the deliverance of Israel from Egypt has a part.

---

*'Jesus Christ is the same yesterday and today and for ever' (Hebrews 13:8).*

JOHN TWISLETON

# The Passover

[The Lord said to Moses and Aaron] You shall keep [the lamb] until the fourteenth day of this month; then the whole assembled congregation of Israel shall slaughter it at twilight. They shall take some of the blood and put it on the two doorposts and the lintel of the houses in which they eat it... This is how you shall eat it: your loins girded, your sandals on your feet, and your staff in your hand; and you shall eat it hurriedly. It is the passover of the Lord. For I will pass through the land of Egypt that night... The blood shall be a sign for you on the houses where you live: when I see the blood, I will pass over you.

I have just been to the Eucharist in a French town where, at the solemn moment, the priest lifted the bread with the words 'Behold the Lamb of God.' As I read this passage in Exodus, I am back in church with Jesus, back with Moses at the Passover, and right back into the heart of God with 'the Lamb who was slain from the creation of the world' (Revelation 13:8, NIV). I am also in heaven around Christ the slain Lamb, as the priest this morning reminded me: 'Blessed are those called to the supper of the Lamb' (see Revelation 19:9).

The sacrifice of Christ the innocent for the guilty is captured by the crucifix, by the lifted bread and wine drawing us to Holy Communion in Christ's body and blood, and by both the unleavened bread and the sacrificial blood of the slaughtered lambs on the doorposts in Exodus 12. God passes over sins through his Son's death 'with the precious blood of Christ, a lamb without blemish or defect' (1 Peter 1:19).

The blood of Christ is a tide flowing down through history. Once revealed on Calvary, its beneficial effects are not limited to Good Friday but reach back to the exodus, giving redemption to Israel, and forward through the Eucharist with its two tables of word and sacrament.

---

*'Behold, the Lamb of God, who takes away the sin of the world!'*
*(John 1:29b, RSV)*

JOHN TWISLETON

# The Festival of Unleavened Bread

[The Lord said to Moses and Aaron] You shall observe the festival of unleavened bread, for on this very day I brought your companies out of the land of Egypt: you shall observe this day throughout your generations as a perpetual ordinance. In the first month, from the evening of the fourteenth day until the evening of the twenty-first day, you shall eat unleavened bread. For seven days no leaven shall be found in your houses; for whoever eats what is leavened shall be cut off from the congregation of Israel, whether an alien or a native of the land. You shall eat nothing leavened; in all your settlements you shall eat unleavened bread.

'You will find the Scriptures enlarge as you enter them,' wrote C.H. Spurgeon. 'The more you study them, the less you will appear to know of them, for they widen out as we approach them.' His comment is relevant to our study of Moses and his institution here of the Festival of Unleavened Bread, or Passover.

'Our paschal lamb, Christ, has been sacrificed. Therefore, let us celebrate the festival, not with the old yeast, the yeast of malice and evil, but with the unleavened bread of sincerity and truth' (1 Corinthians 5:7b–8). Which festival are we talking of—Easter or Passover? They are the same. Old and new covenants are fused in Christ who opens up the way to life and immortality.

If Israel was the firstborn of God's people, her release from physical bondage was as decisive as it is for us in Christ. To eat unleavened bread symbolises repentance—breaking with 'malice and evil'—and faith in the future that Christ brings is symbolised by Israel's promised land. The apostle Paul calls us as urgently as God bade the Israelites to leave Egypt. There can be no waiting for the bread to rise: we are to go forward decisively in 'sincerity and truth'.

---

*Sometimes, spiritual progress is possible only through going back a stage in our lives to deal with resentment, or stopping to cast anxiety upon the Lord. Do I need to take such decisive action?*

JOHN TWISLETON

# Moses and the death of the firstborn

At midnight the Lord struck down all the firstborn in the land of Egypt, from the firstborn of Pharaoh... to the firstborn of the prisoner who was in the dungeon... Pharaoh arose in the night, he and all his officials and all the Egyptians; and there was a loud cry in Egypt, for there was not a house without someone dead. Then he summoned Moses and Aaron in the night, and said, 'Rise up, go away from my people, both you and the Israelites! Go, worship the Lord, as you said. Take your flocks and your herds, as you said, and be gone. And bring a blessing on me too!'

Amid the considerations of theology, literary criticism and symbolism relating to the firstborn, it is the universal loud cry that jumps out at you in reading this difficult section of the life of Moses. It is a terrible sound of tragic, sudden bereavement, matching the cries implied at the start of his story, in the drowning of the Hebrew baby boys (Exodus 1:22).

What spiritual gain can we take from this story? Looking at Moses in the light of Christ, we hear this loud cry in his own death cry on Calvary (Mark 15:34). This, and the loud cry that Jesus made when he called out Lazarus from death (John 11:43), remind us that God in Christ does not stand aloof from the Egyptian tragedy, despite the chilling sense in Exodus 12:29 that the Lord was the author of it.

Another meditation might follow the status of Jesus and believers in him as 'the firstborn' (Romans 8:29), and the Christian interpretation of the work of Moses, who 'by faith... kept the Passover and the sprinkling of blood, so that the destroyer of the firstborn would not touch the firstborn of Israel' (Hebrews 11:28). Through our new birth as Christians, we see scripture with new eyes. 'Those who are spiritual [that is, in receipt of the Holy Spirit] discern all things' (1 Corinthians 2:15).

---

*Come, Holy Spirit, and open the scriptures to us. Take us beyond reason to the realm of your transformative insight, as there is no word of God without power.*

JOHN TWISLETON

# Moses leads the exodus

[Pharaoh] summoned Moses and Aaron in the night, and said, 'Rise up, go away from my people, both you and the Israelites!... The Israelites journeyed from Rameses to Succoth, about six hundred thousand men on foot, besides children. A mixed crowd also went up with them, and livestock in great numbers, both flocks and herds. They baked unleavened cakes of the dough that they had brought out of Egypt; it was not leavened, because they were driven out of Egypt and could not wait, nor had they prepared any provisions for themselves. The time that the Israelites had lived in Egypt was four hundred and thirty years. At the end of four hundred and thirty years, on that very day, all the companies of the Lord went out from the land of Egypt.

The sizeable flow of refugees now arriving in Europe from the Middle East resonates with the immense movement of the Jewish exodus there, around 3000 years ago. That movement 'from Rameses', said to be of around two million people, represented the loss of a high proportion of Egypt's population, a movement not unparalleled in our day from that region.

Historians support the idea of such a movement of workers coming together in Sinai and moving on to Palestine, but the biblical dating carries some ambiguity. Were the 430 years the duration of the Israelites' stay in Egypt or, as in Galatians 3:17, the time from Abraham to Moses? Looking at Moses in the light of Jesus, we see the repeated invitation, from God to his people, into a loving covenant relationship through Abraham, then Moses at Sinai, and finally Jesus.

As God's instrument, Moses freed Israel from slavery. As God's Son, Jesus frees us from sin, sickness, bondage and death in a new exodus that 'leads us in triumphal procession' (2 Corinthians 2:14). Like the Israelites, we experience sin, sickness, bondage and death, but the power of these forces over us has been broken by Christ's triumphant death and resurrection—our source of forgiveness, healing, deliverance and salvation.

---

*Nothing in all creation 'will be able to separate us from the love of God in Christ Jesus our Lord' (Romans 8:39b).*

JOHN TWISLETON

# Moses and the pillars of cloud and fire

Moses took with him the bones of Joseph, who had required a solemn oath of the Israelites, saying, 'God will surely take notice of you, and then you must carry my bones with you from here.' They set out from Succoth, and camped at Etham, on the edge of the wilderness. The Lord went in front of them in a pillar of cloud by day, to lead them along the way, and in a pillar of fire by night, to give them light, so that they might travel by day and by night. Neither the pillar of cloud by day nor the pillar of fire by night left its place in front of the people.

The God of the Bible is a God who reveals himself in history, and the Bible is a record of that revelation. The exodus is seen as God's greatest historical revelation in the Old Testament, with the accompanying manifestations of his presence in these pillars of cloud and fire, directing the forward movement of his people day and night.

In the Easter liturgy, a large candle is lit and carried ahead of the congregation into the dark church as the minister proclaims 'the light of Christ'. This symbolism takes up that of the pillar of fire. At the night vigil, we sing of the creation, the exodus and the resurrection as one action of one God, who continues to lead his people towards the glorious kingdom ahead of us. We look back to Moses, since 'our ancestors were all under the cloud, and all passed through the sea' (1 Corinthians 10:1b), and forward to Christ's redemption, reminding ourselves of its fulfilment on his return.

Just as electricity has expanded the useful hours of the day, so the pillar of fire helped Moses and Israel to follow God day and night. Ironically, the light of Christ today, in my experience, is helping us to recover the best use of his gift of time by disciplining our excessive involvement in electronic media!

---

*'Guide me, O thou great Redeemer... Let the fire and cloudy pillar lead me all my journey through... Be thou still my strength and shield' (William Williams, 1745).*

JOHN TWISLETON

# Moses crosses the Red Sea

Moses stretched out his hand over the sea. The Lord drove the sea back by a strong east wind all night, and turned the sea into dry land; and the waters were divided. The Israelites went into the sea on dry ground, the waters forming a wall for them on their right and on their left. The Egyptians pursued, and went into the sea after them, all of Pharaoh's horses, chariots, and chariot drivers… Moses stretched out his hand over the sea, and at dawn the sea returned to its normal depth. As the Egyptians fled before it, the Lord tossed the Egyptians into the sea.

Walking from Seaford to Eastbourne on the South Downs involves crossing the River Cuckmere either by bridge, which adds two miles, or by walking through it (once you've checked the tide tables). The Israelites had an easier passage and the tide was seen to!

Leading people into God's possibilities requires the upward, forward focus of faith. 'The only limit to the power of Almighty God lies within the individual,' said the famous minister of healing Kathryn Kuhlman, taking inspiration from Moses (*I Believe in Miracles*, Prentice-Hall, 1962, p. 16).

The crossing of the Red Sea has been given natural explanations galore, but we would not still be reflecting upon it if it hadn't been formative for God's people, who are primarily those who put their faith in God and celebrate the consequences. So significant is this Old Testament passage that it gains a mention in the blessing of the water in the Anglican service of baptism: 'Through water you led the children of Israel from slavery in Egypt to freedom in the Promised Land… Sanctify this water… Renewed in your image, may [the baptised] walk by the light of faith' (*Common Worship*).

As they were being pursued by the Egyptians, Moses and his people were driven to put faith in God, with astonishing consequences. By choice, baptised believers walk in the light of faith, knowing that 'a little bit of faith in a great big God works wonders' (Greg Leavers).

---

*'The only limit to the power of Almighty God lies within the individual.'*

JOHN TWISLETON

# The song of Moses

Then Moses and the Israelites sang this song to the Lord: 'I will sing to the Lord, for he has triumphed gloriously; horse and rider he has thrown into the sea. The Lord is my strength and my might, and he has become my salvation; this is my God, and I will praise him, my father's God, and I will exalt him. The Lord is a warrior; the Lord is his name... In your steadfast love you led the people whom you redeemed; you guided them by your strength to your holy abode.'

When we make God our strength, he becomes our song. The struggle of Moses has been made in that strength, and so, having crossed the sea, he bursts into song, which is taken up by Miriam and repeated down the ages. It is a canticle used at Easter time, when the triumph over 'horse and rider, thrown into the sea' is applied to Christ's lifting of the deep waters of death at his resurrection.

'He has become my salvation,' Moses sings. We cannot save ourselves from sin and death; only God can do it for us, when we put faith in him. Military imagery such as 'The Lord is a warrior' may sit uncomfortably with some of us, but it is appropriate for the divine initiative against God's unrepentant enemies. Death, like Pharaoh, is beyond persuasion. Jesus grapples with it at the tomb and overthrows it, so it is 'out at the count'!

We leave the story of Moses for now. His God-given audacity towers over that of everyone else involved in the events of the exodus, in which he served as mediator, representing the underprivileged and speaking truth to power. He was a many-sided personality whose rise in Egypt prepared him for his ascent as a holy man, the founder of three religions. We have read Moses, as only Christians can, as precursor of the new Moses, Jesus Christ, who lifts the veil from the meaning of the Old Testament for those who turn to him (2 Corinthians 3:15–16).

---

*'The law indeed was given through Moses; grace and truth came through Jesus Christ' (John 1:17).*

JOHN TWISLETON

# Atonement: surveying the cross

'When I survey the wondrous cross' has been a popular hymn for centuries. Almost all Christians agree that the cross is central to the good news of Jesus; the Gospels devote almost half their space to the events leading up to it and following it.

But what exactly was accomplished on the cross? Was it, as some think, an unplanned disaster that God put right by the resurrection? Was it the inevitable outcome of Jesus' repeated challenges to the religious and political authorities? Or was it part of God's plan from the very beginning? And how does it 'work'? Precisely how does the death of Jesus atone for, or take away, the sins of the world?

Theologians have debated the meaning of the cross for two millennia, and I don't propose to 'solve' the question in this short series of readings. What I do hope to do is to explore the main theories that have been proposed over the lifetime of the Christian Church and to examine how they relate to the many and varied scriptures about the cross of Christ. On the way, we will encounter some ideas that move us deeply, and perhaps others that leave us cold. In the end, what matters about the cross is that it opens the way for us to renew our relationship with the God and Father of our Lord Jesus Christ. After all, the English word 'atonement' is derived from 'at-one-ment', that which makes us at one with the will of God.

The cross, however, is not just about making individuals right with God. In the last few readings, I will be exploring the fruits of the cross, the results it brings about, not just for those who metaphorically throw themselves at its foot, but for the world that God loved enough to send the Son to redeem it. Finally I will look at an often neglected aspect of the cross—the idea that on the cross Jesus not only died for our sins but identified with, and so redeemed and transformed, all our human sufferings.

VERONICA ZUNDEL

# Expect the unexpected

Jesus went on with his disciples to the villages of Caesarea Philippi; and on the way he asked his disciples, 'Who do people say that I am?' And they answered him, 'John the Baptist; and others, Elijah; and still others, one of the prophets.' He asked them, 'But who do you say that I am?' Peter answered him, 'You are the Messiah.'... Then he began to teach them that the Son of Man must undergo great suffering, and be rejected by the elders, the chief priests, and the scribes, and be killed, and after three days rise again. He said all this quite openly. And Peter took him aside and began to rebuke him. But turning and looking at his disciples, he rebuked Peter and said, 'Get behind me, Satan! For you are setting your mind not on divine things but on human things.'

When someone dies in the prime of life, we tend to see it as 'bad luck' or a tragic accident. What this passage, paralleled in the other Gospels, tells us is that Jesus' death on the cross is no accident. He expects it, and he regards it as necessary: 'The Son of Man must undergo great suffering.' If they had thought of him only as a prophet, the disciples might have suspected that persecution and even death were possible, for 'they persecuted the prophets who were before you' (Matthew 5:12). But the Messiah was not supposed to die. He was supposed to usher in the kingdom of God right away.

What do you do when someone, perhaps a leader in your church, does or says something unexpected that you disagree with? We usually respond like Peter, trying to marshal arguments to the contrary, but are we prepared to entertain the possibility that the other person is right?

Jesus' response, 'Get behind me', may not be just a way of saying 'Go away'; perhaps it indicates that Peter is to put himself in the position of a disciple, following Jesus rather than trying to lead him. We should not follow leaders blindly, but we must be ready to hear and see new things from them.

---

*Pray for the readiness to accept the unexpected, even if it may lead to suffering.*

VERONICA ZUNDEL

# A man called Ransom

When the ten heard this, they began to be angry with James and John. So Jesus called them and said to them, 'You know that among the Gentiles those whom they recognise as their rulers lord it over them, and their great ones are tyrants over them. But it is not so among you; but whoever wishes to become great among you must be your servant, and whoever wishes to be first among you must be slave of all. For the Son of Man came not to be served but to serve, and to give his life a ransom for many.'

As a supporter of Christian Peacemaker Teams, who work for peace in conflict situations, I remember when four members of a delegation were kidnapped and held hostage in Iraq in 2005. Three were freed by the military, but one had already been killed by their captors.

Kidnapping is common in unstable states, and, if ransom demands are made, there is always a debate over whether to pay and 'reward' the kidnappers. Perhaps the oldest way of explaining how Jesus atones for our sins on the cross is the 'ransom' theory. According to this idea, which held sway for a whole millennium, humanity is kept captive in sin and death by Satan, who demands a ransom payment to free us. Jesus' death pays the ransom, but Satan is tricked because Jesus then rises from the dead, effectively receiving the 'ransom'—his life—back again. C.S. Lewis reflected this view of the atonement when he called the hero of his science-fiction trilogy 'Ransom'.

This approach has much biblical support. Its attraction is that it emphasises the ideas of redemption and liberty, suggesting that our freedom in Christ is a real freedom from slavery to sin (see Romans 6:16–18), not just a contractual 'free pass to heaven'.

It is notable that Norman Kember, one of the Christian Peacemaker Teams hostages and a pacifist, felt ambivalent about being freed by the use of violence. Jesus frees us, in contrast, by accepting violence against himself. He rejects any coercive power like that sought by James and John in Mark 10.

---

*'For freedom Christ has set us free. Stand firm, therefore, and do not submit again to a yoke of slavery' (Galatians 5:1).*

VERONICA ZUNDEL

# One for all

I urge that supplications, prayers, intercessions, and thanksgivings should be made for everyone, for kings and all who are in high positions, so that we may lead a quiet and peaceable life in all godliness and dignity. This is right and is acceptable in the sight of God our Saviour, who desires everyone to be saved and to come to the knowledge of the truth. For there is one God; there is also one mediator between God and humankind, Christ Jesus, himself human, who gave himself a ransom for all.

Do you pray for your government? I find it hard, when I disagree with so many of their actions, but Jesus commands us, 'Love your enemies and pray for those who persecute you' (Matthew 5:44). This passage is often used to explore our relationship with 'the powers that be'. However, today another aspect of it strikes me. Did you notice the phrases 'who desires everyone to be saved' and 'a ransom for all'?

Some Christians believe that Jesus died only for a limited number of 'the elect'. I find this idea profoundly unbiblical (although I expect some readers will disagree), given that the words 'everyone' and 'all' are prominent in this part of Paul's letter. I'm not pronouncing on who will be saved, but rather on what the Bible says God wants. As 2 Peter 3:9 puts it, God is 'not willing that any should perish' (KJV). The question is, 'Does God get what God wants?'

The importance of this here is that Jesus' death expressed his sacrificial love, not just for some of humanity but for all (although, of course, not all know or acknowledge it). I find the idea beautifully expressed in one of the Anglican choices for the eucharistic prayer: 'He opened wide his arms for us on the cross.'

Just as all of us are held in thrall to sin and its 'wages', death, so all of us have the option to accept the ransom that Jesus paid on our behalf. To accept it, though, we have to know about it, and that has motivated missionaries and evangelists for millennia.

---

*We are not all called to be evangelists, but we all have opportunities to be witnesses. Pray that you will know the right words to say when the chance comes.*

VERONICA ZUNDEL

# Dying, he destroyed death

And when you were dead in trespasses and the uncircumcision of your flesh, God made you alive together with him, when he forgave us all our trespasses, erasing the record that stood against us with its legal demands. He set this aside, nailing it to the cross. He disarmed the rulers and authorities and made a public example of them, triumphing over them in it.

The Bible is full of paradoxes—apparently self-contradictory but true statements. Some are reflected in words such as Charles Wesley's ''Tis mystery all: the Immortal dies.' Today's passage expresses one central paradox—that Jesus destroyed the power of death by submitting to it.

A historic variant of the 'ransom' theory, given more attention since an influential 20th-century book called *Christus Victor* by Gustav Aulen, is the idea that Jesus' death represents a victory over the 'powers' that rule the earth and our human lives (see also Ephesians 6:12). By this understanding, the resurrection becomes more than a divine 'I told you so'; rather, it represents the paradox that, by dying himself, Jesus conquered death.

Mennonites and other Anabaptists, who are against all use of violence, find this understanding particularly helpful. Some interpretations of the cross risk suggesting that God required violence against God's Son in order to forgive us. But Colossians 2 shows God in the person of the Son taking a non-violent stance, enduring violence himself in order to 'disarm' the powers. In Paul's words in 2 Corinthians 5:19 (KJV): 'God was *in Christ*, reconciling the world unto himself' (italics mine). The powers only understand violence; Jesus undermines them by absorbing their violence into his body.

When people justify using force against offenders by saying, 'It's the only language they understand', I always want to ask, 'Why not teach them another one, then?'

---

*'Everyone who commits sin is a child of the devil… The Son of God was revealed for this purpose, to destroy the works of the devil' (1 John 3:8). Jesus' mission is to destroy everything in the world that is evil, dehumanising and destructive. How can we join him in this?*

VERONICA ZUNDEL

# In our place

For since death came through a human being, the resurrection of the dead has also come through a human being; for as all die in Adam, so all will be made alive in Christ... The first man was from the earth, a man of dust; the second man is from heaven. As was the man of dust, so are those who are of the dust; and as is the man of heaven, so are those who are of heaven. Just as we have borne the image of the man of dust, we will also bear the image of the man of heaven.

Many years ago, I wrote a poem called 'Cross Dressing', in which I portrayed the atonement as Jesus 'swapping clothes' with us, taking on our ragged, dirty outfit and giving us his lordly, beautiful garments made of pure light. So we were transformed from beggars to givers, able to share his generosity with others.

In the poem I was expressing another ancient view of the cross, the idea of 'recapitulation'—that Jesus took on the role of the 'new Adam', or the representative human being, succeeding where Adam failed. Whether or not you believe in a historical Adam and Eve, this suggests that what humanity was unable to do—to live in complete obedience to God—Jesus, both human and divine, did on our behalf. Because of his obedience 'to the point of death' (Philippians 2:8), we can not only be forgiven but can also live a new life of righteousness and justice. As Paul puts it, 'For our sake he made him to be sin who knew no sin, so that in him we might become the righteousness of God' (2 Corinthians 5:21).

I find this view of the atonement sympathetic in that it focuses on how Jesus shares our human experience, becoming like us 'fully human in every way' except sin (Hebrews 2:17, NIV). The famous Grünewald altarpiece at Isenheim in Germany reflects this perspective, showing Jesus on the cross, covered entirely in wounds and sores, just like the patients in the medieval hospital where it was displayed.

---

*As a teenager I often felt I wanted to restart my life and do it properly. It took me years to realise that Jesus had already done it for me. Pray for those who are in despair about their lives.*

VERONICA ZUNDEL

# Paid in full

Every high priest chosen from among mortals is put in charge of things pertaining to God on their behalf, to offer gifts and sacrifices for sins. He is able to deal gently with the ignorant and wayward, since he himself is subject to weakness; and because of this he must offer sacrifice for his own sins as well as for those of the people... Unlike the other high priests, [Jesus] has no need to offer sacrifices day after day, first for his own sins, and then for those of the people; this he did once for all when he offered himself.

When I was 14, impressed by the stance of a friend of about the same age, I went vegetarian. It was partly to do with not wanting animals to be killed, but also, I realise now, a need to 'give something up'; as, at that age I hadn't yet taken up many vices, the only thing I could think of was meat!

We all have an inner impulse, when things go wrong for us, to try to fix them by making some sort of sacrifice, whether to God or to the gurus of slimming or fitness. This impulse goes way back in human history, to the first human who killed an animal not for food but to burn in a religious ceremony—or, biblically speaking, back to Cain and Abel.

It is impossible to understand the cross without the context of the long Old Testament history of grain and animal sacrifices, given to ensure God's favour. The writer of Hebrews notes, however, that none of these religious offerings actually ensured God's forgiveness for the people's sins. The Old Testament itself admits this repeatedly: see, for instance, Psalm 40:6–8, quoted in Hebrews 10:5: 'Sacrifice and offering you do not desire, but you have given me an open ear.'

Hebrews presents Jesus, however, as the perfect and only sufficient sacrifice, which is offered not by the people to God, but by God to the people. This is the basic idea behind the approach to the cross that we will look at tomorrow.

---

*What does it mean to you that Jesus has 'paid for your sins'?*
*What difference does it make to your life?*

VERONICA ZUNDEL

# Honour restored

Yet it was the will of the Lord to crush him with pain. When you make his life an offering for sin, he shall see his offspring, and shall prolong his days; through him the will of the Lord shall prosper. Out of his anguish he shall see light; he shall find satisfaction through his knowledge. The righteous one, my servant, shall make many righteous, and he shall bear their iniquities.

For many Christians, what first attracted them to the faith was being told that Jesus' death cancels out the debt that they owe God because of their sinfulness. It may be a surprise to hear that this understanding did not emerge until 1000 years after Christ, when Anselm of Canterbury wrote his treatise *Cur Deus homo?* or 'Why did God become human?' In it he formulates what has come to be called the 'satisfaction' theory.

Anselm disliked the idea that we owe a ransom to Satan, who is keeping us in bondage; rather, he felt that we owe a debt to God. God's honour is offended by our sin, so the debt of honour to God has to be paid in the death of God's Son. This idea came out of medieval feudalism, in which the lord was owed debts of work or taxes by his workforce. It may still resonate in a society where the whole money system is based on various kinds of debt. However, many Christians find it uncongenial, in that it portrays God as an offended aristocrat who demands satisfaction.

Of course, this is a caricature, and many people still find it liberating to know that, in the words of a song by Christian singer Steve Taylor, God says, 'You owe me nothing.' The problem comes when people insist that this is the only correct interpretation of the cross, especially in its more modern form of 'penal substitution', which we will consider tomorrow.

---

*What attracted you first to the Christian faith? Is this still the core of the faith for you?*

VERONICA ZUNDEL

# Justice is done

But now, apart from law, the righteousness of God has been disclosed, and is attested by the law and the prophets, the righteousness of God through faith in Jesus Christ for all who believe. For there is no distinction, since all have sinned and fall short of the glory of God; they are now justified by his grace as a gift, through the redemption that is in Christ Jesus, whom God put forward as a sacrifice of atonement by his blood, effective through faith. He did this to show his righteousness, because in his divine forbearance he had passed over the sins previously committed; it was to prove at the present time that he himself is righteous and that he justifies the one who has faith in Jesus.

In Auschwitz in 1941, the Franciscan friar Maximilian Kolbe offered to die in place of another prisoner who had a wife and children. Perhaps he was thinking of Jesus' statement, 'No one has greater love than this, to lay down one's life for one's friends' (John 15:13).

How can a just God overlook the injustices that humanity commits? This was the question that led to the idea of 'penal substitution', a development of the 'satisfaction' theory that emerged in the 16th-century Reformation. In this theory, God, to meet the demands of justice, must punish human sin. The punishment, however, would be more than human beings could ever bear. So God, in the person of Jesus, takes the punishment on behalf of humanity. Thus God is shown to be just and yet can forgive our sins without condoning them.

Most people do not need to be told that we are sinful, although we might use other words to describe it, such as failure, self-centredness or inadequacy. In historic revivals, those convicted of the reality of God often spent hours, or even days, emotionally lamenting their sins before they could feel sure that God in Christ had forgiven them. The doctrine of penal substitution has proved liberating for millions, but we need to recognise that some people find more hope and meaning in other approaches to the cross.

---

*Pray that you may experience the reality of God's forgiveness, and so be more able to forgive others.*

VERONICA ZUNDEL

# An example to follow

Therefore, since we are surrounded by so great a cloud of witnesses, let us also lay aside every weight and the sin that clings so closely, and let us run with perseverance the race that is set before us, looking to Jesus the pioneer and perfecter of our faith, who for the sake of the joy that was set before him endured the cross, disregarding its shame, and has taken his seat at the right hand of the throne of God. Consider him who endured such hostility against himself from sinners, so that you may not grow weary or lose heart.

Who are your role models? Since my mother died a few years ago, I have been increasingly realising how much of a role model she was for me. Although not a Christian, she was always kind, generous and ready to try to solve people's problems.

An early model of how the cross 'works', which enjoyed new popularity in the 20th century, was the 'moral influence' theory, in which Jesus' death is an inspiration to us to live loving, 'cross-shaped' lives. It is true that living the kind of life Jesus lived, championing the poor and marginalised and defying the political and religious powers, increases our risk of being in trouble with the authorities and even of being put to death. I think of Rachel Corrie, a young Quaker who stood in front of an Israeli bulldozer to prevent a house demolition, and was run over and killed.

Hebrews exhorts us to follow the self-sacrificing example of Jesus. However, even he could only sacrifice himself because he had a vision of 'the joy that was set before him' (v. 2). The resurrection confirms that love is stronger than death and that God will never abandon those who serve the kingdom.

We are certainly meant to 'imitate Christ', even at the risk of our lives. However, this theory alone is not enough to encompass the rich range of imagery that is used for the cross in the New Testament, drawn from the law courts, the temple, marriage and battle. The cross has many meanings, and this is only one of them.

---

*Which approach to the cross so far has inspired you the most, and why?*

VERONICA ZUNDEL

# Take up your gallows

He called the crowd with his disciples, and said to them, 'If any want to become my followers, let them deny themselves and take up their cross and follow me. For those who want to save their life will lose it, and those who lose their life for my sake, and for the sake of the gospel, will save it. For what will it profit them to gain the whole world and forfeit their life?'

'No one can know Christ in life, unless they follow him,' said one of the Anabaptist reformers. However we interpret the cross, our call is always to respond to it, not only by belief but by the action which is the only real demonstration of faith (see James 2:17–18).

What can it have meant to the disciples, who had not yet seen Jesus die and found it hard to believe that he would, to hear him tell them to 'take up their cross'? It certainly would not have meant something like 'patiently put up with your irritating relative'. The cross was an instrument of torture and execution: to recover the shock of this command, we would have to say 'take up your electric chair' or '... your lethal injection'. Jesus, in fact, is asking us to take up a lifestyle so countercultural that it may get us killed.

In Western society, influenced over millennia by Christian faith and teaching, it is difficult to imagine a situation in which Christians would actually be put to death for their actions. But elsewhere in the world, people motivated by faith have actually been killed for, for instance, standing up for land rights for indigenous peoples. Even in the developed West, people, including Christians, have received death threats for speaking out against injustice. The shadow of the cross has not left our world.

To speak out or stand out is scary. We may get attacked, verbally or even physically, but if God calls us, we need to answer. And those of us who are not called to dangerous dissent need to support and pray for those who are.

---

*Pray for those whose faith leads them to defend the poor and oppressed.*

VERONICA ZUNDEL

# Us and them

Remember that you were at that time without Christ, being aliens from the commonwealth of Israel, and strangers to the covenants of promise, having no hope and without God in the world. But now in Christ Jesus you who once were far off have been brought near by the blood of Christ. For he is our peace; in his flesh he has made both groups into one and has broken down the dividing wall, that is, the hostility between us. He has abolished the law with its commandments and ordinances, that he might create in himself one new humanity in place of the two, thus making peace, and might reconcile both groups to God in one body through the cross, thus putting to death that hostility through it.

One of my favourite sayings is 'There are two kinds of people in the world: those who divide the world into two kinds of people, and those who do not.' I'm afraid most of us are in the first group. Human society often functions by identifying a group of 'them' out there, who are different from 'us' and with whom we should have nothing to do.

For first-century Jews, 'they' were the Gentiles, seen as lawless and ungodly. Because, in Christ, we are made righteous by God's grace rather than by following the Jewish law, that distinction is broken down. As we begin to look at the results of Jesus' cross, we see that it goes much further than saving individuals from destruction. It has a social effect, uniting in Jesus those who have been locked into mutual hostility.

For the last 23 years I've been in a church that, for historic reasons, was socially monochrome, consisting mainly of white, educated, middle-class people. Normally, though, a church should be a place where people with all sorts of backgrounds, ethnic origins and abilities are united in experiencing the grace of God and in following Jesus. We can only make this diverse community work by treating the 'weakest members' with the greatest respect (see 1 Corinthians 12:22–23). (This does not, of course, mean that some members should use the claim of weakness to dominate all the others!)

---

*How have you seen Christ uniting conflicting groups?*

VERONICA ZUNDEL

# The cross and creation

He is the image of the invisible God, the firstborn of all creation; for in him all things in heaven and on earth were created, things visible and invisible, whether thrones or dominions or rulers or powers – all things have been created through him and for him. He himself is before all things, and in him all things hold together. He is the head of the body, the church; he is the beginning, the firstborn from the dead, so that he might come to have first place in everything. For in him all the fullness of God was pleased to dwell, and through him God was pleased to reconcile to himself all things, whether on earth or in heaven, by making peace through the blood of his cross.

'Nothing is lost, and all in the end is harvest,' wrote the poet Edith Sitwell. We tend to focus on Jesus' cross as a way of making it possible for human beings to be reconciled to God, but God's plan is much greater than that. By shedding his blood on the cross, Jesus opened the way for the whole of creation to be reconciled to God.

Just as human sinfulness leads to disruption in human relationships, in our relationship to creation and in creation itself (see Genesis 3:14–19), so the offering of Christ, the perfect human, has begun the reversal of the process. Now 'all things' (not just 'some people') can be brought back to their true selves. C.S. Lewis portrays it beautifully in his book *The Last Battle*, where 'the true Narnia' is revealed in all its glory.

Our destiny in Christ is not to be whisked away to some ethereal heaven to sit on clouds and play harps; it is to live for ever in a new, transformed creation that works the way God intended it to work. In our lives today, which are often so hard, we can still get glimpses of that new creation—for example, in the beauty of a landscape or a gesture of love between people. We can also care for the present creation and its inhabitants, in honour of what it will become.

---

*Creator God, give me a vision of what it means for all things to be reconciled.*

VERONICA ZUNDEL

# Like a lamb

Then I saw between the throne and the four living creatures and among the elders a Lamb standing as if it had been slaughtered… He went and took the scroll from the right hand of the one who was seated on the throne. When he had taken the scroll, the four living creatures and the twenty-four elders fell before the Lamb… They sing a new song: 'You are worthy to take the scroll and to open its seals, for you were slaughtered and by your blood you ransomed for God saints from every tribe and language and people and nation; you have made them to be a kingdom and priests serving our God, and they will reign on earth.'

'Like a lamb led to the slaughter' is not a phrase we normally use to describe a good situation. We say it of someone whose innocence has allowed them to be exploited or abused. Yet here in John's vision of ultimate reality, we see Jesus, not as a devouring lion coming to judge the world but as a tender lamb who has fallen prey to the slaughterer. So the cross was not a 'gateway to power', to be left behind with Jesus' earthly life; rather, it expresses the core nature of God's love for us. Jesus is for ever the crucified one, bearing the scars of his suffering.

We speak and sing of Jesus as Lord and king, and so he is, but he is a king with scars, a king who does not merely sit on the throne but stands humbly next to it. Not only this, but it is the fact that his scars are still visible that makes him 'worthy to take the scroll'—that is, to interpret human history and bring it to its fulfilment.

What about ourselves? Far from boasting of how God protects us from all harm, perhaps we should instead be willing to earn our stripes by the way we survive suffering (see 2 Corinthians 4:7–12). Indeed, experience tells us that it is often those who have had the hardest lives who are the most filled with Jesus' compassion.

---

*'For I decided to know nothing among you except Jesus Christ, and him crucified' (1 Corinthians 2:2).*

VERONICA ZUNDEL

# The other half of the gospel

Surely he has borne our infirmities and carried our diseases; yet we accounted him stricken, struck down by God, and afflicted. But he was wounded for our transgressions, crushed for our iniquities; upon him was the punishment that made us whole, and by his bruises we are healed. All we like sheep have gone astray; we have all turned to our own way, and the Lord has laid on him the iniquity of us all.

Even if we disagree about exactly what the cross means, 'Jesus died for our sins' is the shortest and most popular formulation of the gospel. However, I believe that it leaves out not only what Jesus lived for and was raised for, but also an often-forgotten 'other half' of what he died for.

If we look at the state of the world, it is quite clear that many of the world's people, not just on the other side of the world but often close to hand and throughout history, have been and are 'more sinned against than sinning'. What of the women who are beaten, abused and eventually killed by their partners? (This group includes at least one known to me since childhood.) What of the child born with a terminal degenerative disease? What of the civilians killed in bombing raids in the last century? How does the cross apply to them?

This passage from Isaiah, which the evangelist Philip used to share the good news with an Ethiopian eunuch (Acts 8:26–39), suggests another dimension of the cross. Certainly it declares that the person prophesied about here (Philip, like many others since, applied it to Jesus) is taking the consequences of our failings. But there is also a strong message that in his life and death he was carrying our sufferings. By his death he conquered sin and death, but he also conquered the many ways in which we endure pain, infirmity and weakness.

Sin and sickness, oppression and exploitation still exist, but on the cross their power is broken.

---

*'Where, O death, is your victory? Where, O death, is your sting?' (1 Corinthians 15:55). Pray that this may be true for yourself or anyone you know who is suffering.*

VERONICA ZUNDEL

# The life and legacy of Solomon

Authors of biographies often adopt a particular angle. The result is that, rather than meeting the genuine person, 'warts and all', we discover a caricature—hero or villain, saint or sinner, role model or 'a lesson to us all'. Biblical character studies can fall into the same trap. However, when we search the scriptures to understand Solomon, the volume and diversity of sources defy any simplistic generalisations.

What we know of Solomon is spread throughout multiple books of several genres. It originates from the quills of a variety of authors, including that of the king himself. To examine the evidence of Solomon's life requires us to engage with history, poetry and wisdom, and what emerges is a multifaceted picture. He was, by any standards, a remarkable man. However, his life displays both faithfulness and rebellion, integrity and deceit. In terms of prosperity and genius, he has few peers in world history, but the scriptures also reveal shortcomings that are common to us all.

Solomon, third king of Israel and son of David and Bathsheba (2 Samuel 12:24–25), was the first to inherit that responsibility and the last to rule over a united Israel. After his 40-year rule ended in 931BC, his name continued to be a byword for wisdom and magnificence. When Jesus wanted to draw a comparison with someone of profound insight or great splendour, he referred to Solomon (Matthew 6:29; 12:42).

Despite his brilliance, Solomon is usually portrayed as a ruler who began in wisdom but ended in folly; one who started well but whose character was eroded by foolish alliances and compromises. His reign is depicted as a dazzling rise followed by a disastrous decline. However, closer inspection reveals both that signs of weakness were visible from earliest times and that his wisdom outlived him.

Solomon's legacy reflects his life: his performance as a ruler was mixed and, while fruits of his wisdom are still with us, his actions sowed the seeds of disaffection that split the kingdom. In his life we find characteristics to emulate and errors to avoid; in his reign we encounter the God of history, eager to fulfil his covenant with David's successor and longing for a people who will walk in his ways.

STEVE AISTHORPE

# What's in a name?

Then David comforted his wife Bathsheba, and he went to her and made love to her. She gave birth to a son, and they named him Solomon. The Lord loved him; and because the Lord loved him, he sent word through Nathan the prophet to name him Jedidiah. Meanwhile Joab fought against Rabbah of the Ammonites and captured the royal citadel. Joab then sent messengers to David, saying, '... Muster the rest of the troops and besiege the city and capture it. Otherwise I will take the city, and it will be named after me.'

In Shakespeare's *Romeo and Juliet*, the protagonists bear the names of two feuding families, Montague and Capulet. Distraught that their relationship may be doomed because of this enmity, Juliet utters the words, 'What's in a name? That which we call a rose by any other name would smell as sweet' (Act II, Scene 2, lines 1–2). Her suggestion is that a name is superficial, just a means of identification.

Living in an era when changing one's name is an administrative formality and names go in and out of fashion, it is difficult for us to grasp the profound meaning attached to names in former times and in other cultures. In the scriptures we find that names are packed with significance. In the case of Solomon (meaning 'peaceful'), there was a prophetic quality to his naming. It spoke of the circumstances of his conception and anticipated his character and influence. After David's tragic downward spiral into adultery, deception and murder, and the anguish of losing a child (2 Samuel 11:1—12:23), the birth of Solomon marked the dawn of a period of personal peace. In contrast to the endless military campaigns of David, Solomon's reign was remarkably peaceable; his subjects 'lived in safety, everyone under their own vine and under their own fig-tree' (1 Kings 4:25).

In sending his prophet to convey another name for Solomon, God indicated his astounding and unending grace. Despite the unsavoury aspects of his heritage, the Lord gave him the name Jedidiah, which translates as 'loved by God' and conveys his ultimate identity.

---

*We share the identity of Solomon: 'For we know, brothers and sisters loved by God, that he has chosen you' (1 Thessalonians 1:4).*

STEVE AISTHORPE

# Big shoes to fill

When the time drew near for David to die, he gave a charge to Solomon his son. 'I am about to go the way of all the earth,' he said. 'So be strong, act like a man, and observe what the Lord your God requires: walk in obedience to him, and keep his decrees and commands, his laws and regulations, as written in the Law of Moses. Do this so that you may prosper in all you do and wherever you go and that the Lord may keep his promise to me: "If your descendants watch how they live, and if they walk faithfully before me with all their heart and soul, you will never fail to have a successor on the throne of Israel."'

It is never easy to follow in the wake of a successful, well-liked or prestigious predecessor. It is harder still if that esteemed forerunner is your own father. Despite his failings, David left an extraordinary legacy. From humble beginnings as shepherd-boy and lackey to his older brothers, he rose to the pre-eminent position of power. His military accomplishments were legendary. His 40-year reign was a period of expansion. As well as being a conquering hero, he was magnanimous towards those he defeated, renowned for his justice and loyal to his friends. He wrote psalms that enriched the worship life of his subjects and have been a blessing to believers in every generation since.

By any standards, Solomon was called to fill the most colossal shoes imaginable. However, as David passed the burden of control from his own elderly shoulders to those of his son, he also shared with him the essential foundation for effective leadership of God's people. In today's passage we are privileged to eavesdrop on David's final words to his son. Drawing on long years of hard-won experience, and longing for his son to uphold and exceed his own accomplishments, David uttered words of advice. The key to exemplary leading, he told Solomon, is faithful following.

*Almighty God, I may not be leading a great nation but I do long to please you in all I think, do and say. Please strengthen my resolve to 'walk faithfully before you with all my heart and soul'. Amen*

STEVE AISTHORPE

# Called and equipped

That night God appeared to Solomon and said to him, 'Ask for whatever you want me to give you.' Solomon answered God, 'You have shown great kindness to David my father and have made me king in his place. Now, Lord God, let your promise to my father David be confirmed, for you have made me king over a people who are as numerous as the dust of the earth. Give me wisdom and knowledge, that I may lead this people, for who is able to govern this great people of yours?' God said to Solomon, 'Since this is your heart's desire and you have not asked for wealth, possessions or honour, nor for the death of your enemies, and since you have not asked for a long life but for wisdom and knowledge to govern my people over whom I have made you king, therefore wisdom and knowledge will be given you.'

History is peppered with accounts of military campaigns, polar expeditions and all kinds of well-meaning ventures that ended in failure and humiliation due to a lack of resources. Faced with an undertaking of immense scope and importance, Solomon knew that he could not prevail alone and unaided. He knew too that only God could provide all he needed, and so he summoned the people to the tent of the Lord's presence and led them in an extravagant act of national worship (2 Chronicles 1:1–6). 'That night' (v. 7), when the buzz and chatter of the crowds had faded and with the aromas of the day's sacrifices lingering in the air, the Lord came to Solomon in a dream and asked, 'What do you want?'

Just as in Jesus' encounter with a blind man, when he asked the very same question (Mark 10:51), the 'right' answer may seem obvious to those of us with the benefit of hindsight. However, we should not underestimate the temptation involved when the almighty creator apparently offers a blank cheque. Solomon would not have been the first or the last person in high public office to seek personal gain, but he did not. Solomon asked wisely and God responded in superabundance.

---

*'Now may the God of peace… equip you with everything good for doing his will' (Hebrews 13:20–21).*

STEVE AISTHORPE

# The king evokes praise and adoration

God gave Solomon wisdom and very great insight, and a breadth of understanding as measureless as the sand on the seashore. Solomon's wisdom was greater than the wisdom of all the people of the East, and greater than all the wisdom of Egypt. He was wiser than anyone else, including Ethan the Ezrahite—wiser than Heman, Kalkol and Darda, the sons of Mahol. And his fame spread to all the surrounding nations. He spoke three thousand proverbs and his songs numbered a thousand and five.

It is intriguing to speculate about the identity of the four outstanding people recorded as those whom King Solomon exceeded in wisdom. With the exception of Ethan the Ezrahite, we know almost nothing about them. In Ethan's case, Psalm 89 is attributed to him and affords us a glimpse of a man who was passionate in faith, ruthless in honesty and eloquent in articulating human emotion. Despite our limited information, we can reasonably assume that these four men were household names, the Nobel Prize laureates of their day. Their presence here adds further emphasis to the writer's assessment of Solomon.

We will soon discover that Solomon was not faultless. However, it is important to recognise him as one of the most dazzlingly brilliant men of history. Each year, *Forbes* magazine publishes a list of the world's most powerful people. There is no doubt that Solomon would have topped such a list year after year. Not only was he a man of rare talent, but his wealth, influence and renown were unparalleled. Although he requested wisdom rather than prosperity (2 Chronicles 1:11–12), the Lord also provided him with material wealth.

While we have a sense of the wonder that Solomon's magnificence aroused, we do well to reflect on the comparison that another 'son of David' (Matthew 1:1)—his descendant, Jesus Christ—drew between this outstanding man and himself when he said, 'Something greater than Solomon is here' (Matthew 12:42).

---

*As the splendour of Solomon caused a visiting Arabian queen to exclaim, 'Praise be to the Lord your God' (2 Chronicles 9:8), how much more should our knowledge of Jesus evoke praise and adoration?*

STEVE AISTHORPE

# An act of worship

Solomon had seventy thousand carriers and eighty thousand stonecutters in the hills, as well as thirty-three hundred foremen who supervised the project and directed the workers. At the king's command they removed from the quarry large blocks of high-grade stone to provide a foundation of dressed stone for the temple. The craftsmen of Solomon and Hiram and workers from Byblos cut and prepared the timber and stone for the building of the temple… The temple that King Solomon built for the Lord was sixty cubits long, twenty wide and thirty high. The portico at the front of the main hall of the temple extended the width of the temple… and projected ten cubits from the front.

David envisaged a temple worthy of the Lord's name. He made extensive preparations for it. However, as a man with blood on his hands, he forfeited the privilege of building it (1 Chronicles 22). Instead, the Lord swore to give that honour to his son, a promise that David conveyed to Solomon and proclaimed publicly (1 Chronicles 28—29).

The construction of the temple was never just about providing a place of worship. The process itself was to be an act of worship, the fruit of Solomon's 'wholehearted devotion' (1 Chronicles 29:19). By modern standards, the dimensions of the temple are unimpressive and the labour involved seems out of proportion to its modest scale. However, as an expression of adoration, every intricate detail was crafted with painstaking precision from the finest materials. To preserve an uninterrupted ambiance of reverence, no hammers or chisels were used at the temple site, each stone being finished to perfection at the quarry to enable a perfect fit (1 Kings 6:7).

Sir Christopher Wren, visiting the construction site of St Paul's Cathedral, asked each craftsman what they were doing. Most replied by describing the immediate task at hand. However, one worker answered, 'I am building a great cathedral for my God.' For him, the mundane had become an act of worship.

---

*What in your life could be transformed into an act of worship by a change of perspective—a decision to do it well for the glory of God?*

STEVE AISTHORPE

# As in private, so in public

Then Solomon stood before the altar of the Lord in front of the whole assembly of Israel, spread out his hands toward heaven and said: 'Lord, the God of Israel, there is no God like you in heaven above or on earth below—you who keep your covenant of love with your servants who continue wholeheartedly in your way. You have kept your promise to your servant David my father; with your mouth you have promised and with your hand you have fulfilled it—as it is today.'

With David as his father, we can assume that Solomon was mentored in the life of prayer. He would have been aware of the prayers that we know from the book of Psalms, including appeals for help, hymns of devotion, cries for mercy, and exclamations of genuine repentance. Here were honest Godward responses for every circumstance. So when Solomon's encounter with God at Gibeon (1 Kings 3:4–5) gives us a first glimpse of the king at prayer, it is no surprise that we witness a petition of childlike trust and humble reverence.

In today's passage we see that out of that private devotion emerged a public persona rooted in dependence on God, and a style of leadership centred on prayer. Having addressed the crowd, blessing them in the name of the Lord and testifying to God's faithfulness, Solomon turned to God. Then, in an inspirational and stirring prayer, he led the people into an awareness of the Lord's presence and providence, pouring out adoration to the one and only, loving, covenant-keeping God. Rather than indulging in self-congratulation for an incredible feat achieved, he directed all praise and honour to 'the Lord our God'.

This is recorded as the day of the dedication of the temple. However, it was also the occasion of a king and his people consecrating themselves to their Lord. From Solomon's closing intercession it appears that he was, like his father, 'a man after God's own heart' (Acts 13:22).

---

*Solomon's words offer a powerful prayer of rededication for us too: 'May he keep us centred and devoted to him, following the life path he has cleared, watching the signposts, walking at the pace and rhythms he laid down for our ancestors' (1 Kings 8:58, The Message).*

STEVE AISTHORPE

# Tested and found wanting

She said to the king, 'The report I heard in my own country about your achievements and your wisdom is true. But I did not believe these things until I came and saw with my own eyes. Indeed, not even half was told me; in wisdom and wealth you have far exceeded the report I heard. How happy your people must be! How happy your officials, who continually stand before you and hear your wisdom!... And she gave the king 120 talents of gold, large quantities of spices, and precious stones. Never again were so many spices brought in as those the queen of Sheba gave to King Solomon.

It all started so well. To all appearances, Solomon was a person of integrity and commitment. He was soon reigning over a united kingdom, where people benefited from security and prosperity. However, a promising beginning is no guarantee of a successful conclusion.

Austerity and adversity present taxing ordeals, but Solomon faced even tougher trials. Perhaps the most demanding tests in terms of maintaining perspective are prosperity and praise, and Solomon had both in abundance. He accumulated treasures at an alarming rate and praise was lavished on him. Wealth can be a blessing when managed wisely. However, as Solomon's own proverbs highlight, riches need to be recognised as a gift from God and used to bring blessing to others (Proverbs 10:22; 11:25). Likewise, praise can provide positive and necessary encouragement, but, just like wealth, it needs to be handled with care: 'Fire tests the purity of silver and gold, but a person is tested by being praised' (Proverbs 27:21, NLT).

No doubt, listening to David's counsel at the outset of his rule, to 'walk in obedience to [God], and keep his decrees and commands' (1 Kings 2:3), Solomon was committed to a lifetime of obedience. However, as the royal coffers overflowed and as he began to accept the acclaim that flooded in, flaws began to appear in his character.

*Ironically, one of the important lessons we can take from Solomon's life is best expressed in a proverb attributed to him: 'Above all else, guard your heart, for everything you do flows from it' (Proverbs 4:23). What might that mean for you?*

STEVE AISTHORPE

# Calamitous compromises

On a hill east of Jerusalem, Solomon built a high place for Chemosh the detestable god of Moab, and for Molek the detestable god of the Ammonites. He did the same for all his foreign wives, who burned incense and offered sacrifices to their gods. The Lord became angry with Solomon because his heart had turned away from the Lord, the God of Israel, who had appeared to him twice... So the Lord said to Solomon, 'Since this is your attitude and you have not kept my covenant and my decrees, which I commanded you, I will most certainly tear the kingdom away from you and give it to one of your subordinates.'

As I write this, the closure of the Forth Road Bridge is causing traffic chaos in Scotland. This spectacular span of steel and concrete has maintained its structural integrity for five decades, but now, because of a two-centimetre hairline crack, it is closed for renovation. While many drivers are frustrated by the lengthy diversions, they are also grateful for the careful regime of checks that has detected the problem and enabled timely repairs.

Even the most sudden downturn is rarely as unpredictable as it first appears. When economic collapses, health crises and relationship breakdowns are considered in retrospect, invariably there were warning signs. So in the life of Solomon, character flaws and compromises gave forewarning of future problems. Keen to forge strategic alliances, he entered into marriages of convenience. Despite the fact that God had forbidden marriage with people of other religions (Deuteronomy 7:1–11), Solomon wagered that the diplomatic advantages of marrying Pharaoh's daughter would justify a one-off concession.

However, just as hairline cracks, if unaddressed, become gaping rifts, so Solomon's first compromise led to many others (1 Kings 11:1–3). In time, the Lord was no longer the sole focus of devotion for him or the nation. He would have done well to follow the monitoring routine of his father: 'Search me, God, and know my heart... See if there is any offensive way in me' (Psalm 139:23–24).

---

*Use this prayer today to invite the Lord to turn his loving and holy gaze on to different aspects of your life.*

STEVE AISTHORPE

# Exploitation and duplicity

At the end of twenty years, during which Solomon built these two buildings—the temple of the Lord and the royal palace—King Solomon gave twenty towns in Galilee to Hiram king of Tyre, because Hiram had supplied him with all the cedar and juniper and gold he wanted. But when Hiram went from Tyre to see the towns that Solomon had given him, he was not pleased with them. 'What kind of towns are these you have given me, my brother?' he asked.

We might assume that leading Israel into a period of unprecedented prosperity and implementing breathtaking building projects would have guaranteed Solomon the loyalty of his people. However, as well as recording Solomon's accomplishments, the scriptures detail the means by which they were achieved—and, sadly, we find that his impressive endeavours sometimes came at an excessive and unjust cost. So intent was Solomon on pursuing his extravagant programme of building works that he was prepared to gamble the well-being and loyalty of his subjects and to sacrifice friendship and reputation.

Slavery and forced labour, especially among conquered peoples, were common practices in the ancient world. However, when foreign labour proved inadequate for Solomon's ambitious plans, he conscripted his own people, taking them away from their livelihoods for a third of the year with no compensation (1 Kings 5:13–17).

Solomon's dealings with the king of Tyre demonstrate his willingness to carve up the kingdom and his readiness to deceive. When Hiram inspected the towns given to him in return for building materials, he found that he had been cheated—and one can only imagine how the people who had been 'sold off' for the sake of Solomon's ambitions must have felt. Forced labour and deception seemed useful but eventually led to a festering resentment that would split the kingdom. We too make choices about who pays the price of our aspirations. The cheapest deals can seem attractive, but we do well to ensure that we are not supporting exploitation or duplicity.

---

*Think about how to ensure that your choices do not lead to the mistreatment of people or the environment.*

STEVE AISTHORPE

# The bigger picture

About that time Jeroboam was going out of Jerusalem, and Ahijah the prophet of Shiloh met him on the way, wearing a new cloak... Ahijah took hold of the new cloak he was wearing and tore it into twelve pieces. Then he said to Jeroboam, 'Take ten pieces for yourself, for this is what the Lord, the God of Israel, says: "See, I am going to tear the kingdom out of Solomon's hand and give you ten tribes. But for the sake of my servant David and the city of Jerusalem, which I have chosen out of all the tribes of Israel, he will have one tribe. I will do this because they have forsaken me and worshipped Ashtoreth the goddess of the Sidonians, Chemosh the god of the Moabites, and Molek the god of the Ammonites, and have not walked in obedience to me, nor done what is right in my eyes, nor kept my decrees and laws as David, Solomon's father, did."'

Solomon's achievements were impressive. Indeed, if the Bible recorded only his accomplishments, we might place the blame for the disintegration of the kingdom at the feet of his successors. However, the Old Testament also provides insights into Solomon's attitudes and methods, and enables us to see his life in the wider scheme of God's intentions.

While God is unequivocally faithful in his covenant with David and his descendants, there is a bigger picture. God is not primarily on the side of this or that tribe. Rebellion against his ways has no role in achieving his purposes. God's patience is staggering and, when people wake up to their wrongdoing, he is eager to redeem and restore (1 John 1:9). However, when those entrusted with his purposes persist in behaviour unworthy of his name, he has no choice but to find others to serve him. Jeroboam is known as someone who rebelled against King Solomon. However, in reality he was one of several people whom the Lord 'raised up' in response to Solomon's disobedience (1 Kings 11:14, 23).

---

*Respond in prayer to the fact that, as in Solomon's day, the Lord is searching for people who will 'walk in his ways' and reflect his glorious character.*

STEVE AISTHORPE

# The perils of accumulation

Then the king made a great throne covered with ivory and overlaid with fine gold. The throne had six steps, and its back had a rounded top. On both sides of the seat were armrests, with a lion standing beside each of them. Twelve lions stood on the six steps, one at either end of each step. Nothing like it had ever been made for any other kingdom. All King Solomon's goblets were gold, and all the household articles in the Palace of the Forest of Lebanon were pure gold. Nothing was made of silver, because silver was considered of little value in Solomon's days. The king had a fleet of trading ships at sea along with the ships of Hiram. Once every three years it returned, carrying gold, silver and ivory, and apes and baboons.

Solomon controlled the gateway for trade between Asia and Egypt. Also, through his alliance with King Hiram, he attained a monopoly of key shipping routes. Rather than using his power to facilitate healthy trading relationships, though, he exerted his influence to put a stranglehold on the region's commercial life.

Undoubtedly, Solomon used the strategic location of Israel, his ability to forge coalitions and his shrewd business sense to bring enormous material gains to Israel. Unfortunately, however, these benefits were far from equally distributed. The iniquitous gap that developed between the rich and poor, which Amos and Micah later denounced, had its origins in Solomon's opulent reign.

At some point, Solomon's passion for trade morphed into a hunger to accumulate, and it led him into further areas of compromise. Despite the Lord's prohibition on acquiring 'great numbers of horses' and the clear command not to 'make the people return to Egypt to get more' (Deuteronomy 17:16), King Solomon did both (1 Kings 10:26). Likewise, the instruction to 'not accumulate large amounts of silver and gold' (Deuteronomy 17:17) was ignored to such a degree that silver became 'as common in Jerusalem as stones' (1 Kings 10:27).

---

*Rather than being content with his considerable wealth, Solomon developed a desire to amass more. We live in a culture where that same craving is actively encouraged. Pray for God's help to escape its grip.*

STEVE AISTHORPE

# The consequences of oppression

The king [Rehoboam] answered the people harshly. Rejecting the advice given him by the elders, he followed the advice of the young men and said, 'My father made your yoke heavy; I will make it even heavier. My father scourged you with whips; I will scourge you with scorpions.' So the king did not listen to the people, for this turn of events was from the Lord, to fulfil the word the Lord had spoken to Jeroboam… When all Israel saw that the king refused to listen to them, they answered the king: 'What share do we have in David, what part in Jesse's son? To your tents, Israel! Look after your own house, David!'

There is a momentum in human institutions, including nations, which means that some of the fruit of wise leadership is enjoyed by successors. Likewise, by the time the full consequences of reckless governance are felt, it is sometimes others who reap what their predecessors sowed. To understand the impact of Solomon's character and actions, we need to look beyond his death and examine both the immediate fallout of his rule and his long-term legacies.

Over the coming days, we will look at some of Solomon's enduring legacies, but today's passage explains how his severe policies, followed by the stubborn callousness of his son, Rehoboam, led to the fragmentation of the kingdom. The people's request for him to 'lighten the harsh labour and the heavy yoke' imposed by Solomon was accompanied with the offer of their dependable service (1 Kings 12:4). Despite the counsel of elders that a charitable response would secure the loyalty of his subjects, Rehoboam preferred to follow the ruthless recommendation of his peers and threatened his citizens with even more punitive policies.

The young king was foolish, but it was not his recklessness alone that caused the break-up of the kingdom. Rather, his uncaring and vindictive response was just one repressive act too many. How ironic it is that what Rehoboam needed to hear, to avert the fallout of Solomon's overbearing rule, was his father's advice: 'A gentle answer turns away wrath, but a harsh word stirs up anger' (Proverbs 15:1).

---

*Pray for grace and courage to choose the gentle response.*

STEVE AISTHORPE

# A legacy of love

Under the apple tree I roused you; there your mother conceived you, there she who was in labour gave you birth. Place me like a seal over your heart, like a seal on your arm; for love is as strong as death, its jealousy unyielding as the grave. It burns like blazing fire, like a mighty flame. Many waters cannot quench love; rivers cannot sweep it away. If one were to give all the wealth of one's house for love, it would be utterly scorned.

In our era of chronic short-sightedness, when football managers are judged on their performance over just a few games, it is good to be reminded that some consequences of a person's life endure for years, decades and centuries. In these final two days reflecting on Solomon, we turn to the legacy that remains with us through his writing. Among his contributions to our Bibles are substantial parts of the book of Proverbs, portions of the Psalms, Solomon's Song of Songs (as it is termed in Hebrew) and Ecclesiastes.

The term 'Song of Songs' is a Hebrew way of saying 'the greatest song of all'. Many have tried to explain why this exquisite and poetic gem is in the scriptures. It has been suggested that it may be an allegory of God's love for Israel and Christ's love for the Church. However, there is no need for a convoluted explanation as to why a celebration of human love resides in God's written word.

The closest parallels to this love poem within scripture are found in Proverbs, where passages within the opening chapters use similar lyrical language to commend and rejoice in wisdom. We should not be surprised to find two of the Lord's most priceless gifts being celebrated in such extravagant fashion.

Today's passage represents the poem's crescendo. It expresses the supreme power of love: 'unyielding as the grave… rivers cannot wash it away' (vv. 6–7). Love's incomparable worth is underscored. The image of a seal speaks of exclusivity and faithfulness, a powerful theme throughout the Song, reiterated in Proverbs (see 3:3) and celebrated in the Psalms as integral to true love (Psalm 85:10).

---

*Lord, please develop in me your powerful, priceless and faithful love.*

STEVE AISTHORPE

# A legacy of wisdom

Unless the Lord builds the house, the builders labour in vain. Unless the Lord watches over the city, the guards stand watch in vain. In vain you rise early and stay up late, toiling for food to eat—for he grants sleep to those he loves. Children are a heritage from the Lord, offspring a reward from him. Like arrows in the hands of a warrior are children born in one's youth. Blessed is the man whose quiver is full of them. They will not be put to shame when they contend with their opponents in court.

We cannot know for sure how many of the more than 1000 songs that Solomon wrote (1 Kings 4:32) made it into the precious collection that we now know as the book of Psalms. However, the clearest attribution to him is attached to Psalm 127. Comprising one of 15 psalms (120—134) known collectively as the Songs of Ascent, Solomon's reminder of the Lord's provision of security (v. 1), rest and sustenance (v. 2) and family (v. 3) formed part of a liturgy used by travellers making pilgrimage to Jerusalem. In a clear and uncomplicated way, Solomon articulates one of the most profound Christian doctrines—the sovereignty of God. Ultimately, Solomon realised, God is king.

The opening verse of Psalm 127 is one of the best-known and most-loved phrases from the Psalter. That simple opening statement, 'Unless the Lord builds the house, the builders labour in vain', expresses with simple eloquence the profound truth that, while all kinds of impressive human achievements are possible, only that which is inspired and enabled by the Creator himself has eternal significance and security.

Perhaps, if the wisdom of Solomon is encapsulated in any one place, we find it in the opening stanza of this psalm. We can imagine it originating from the musings of the elderly king as he reflected on his reign—with gratitude to the Lord for many blessings and with remorse for the folly of his own attempts to stage-manage events.

*This insight of Solomon is echoed in the teaching of Jesus. Reflect on his words, 'If you remain in me and I in you, you will bear much fruit; apart from me you can do nothing' (John 15:5).*

STEVE AISTHORPE

# Anger

Please don't be put off by the subject of the next fortnight's readings! Anyone reading the Bible will be aware that 'anger' is a word frequently found, describing human anger and even, sometimes to our surprise, divine anger. We are all aware of what anger is and every single one of us has experienced it—the steady rise of internal temperature until boiling point is reached and it explodes in angry words or even, sadly, violent actions. That's human anger, and the Bible has plenty to say about it and how it can be 'managed', as we shall see. It's ugly, regrettable and shameful. We know that, of course. But when the red mist descends, it is sometimes hard to remember that Christians are called to be peacemakers and to 'live in love and peace with all'.

God's anger is often described in the Old Testament (the Hebrew scriptures, the Bible of Jesus) as being 'kindled'. In other words, it has a cause. Something lights the fire—and it's always a human firelighter. Sometimes God's anger at sin and sinners is called 'wrath', a slightly different version of much the same thing. What bothers us, when we read of this anger, is that we prefer to think of God as a God of love. 'God is love,' we mutter, 'so what's he doing being angry?'

We shall look at several instances in which God's anger or wrath are provoked, but the fundamental answer to that worrying question lies not in individual cases but in the very nature of God. The most frequent word used in the scriptures to describe God's nature—its constant presence disguised by various translations of the same word—is the Hebrew word *chesdh*. It's a beautiful word for a beautiful idea—loving kindness, steadfast love, faithful love—and yet it constantly turns up in the scriptures, especially in the Psalms, alongside references to God's anger at sin and his judgement of sinners. Like the mother who gets angry with her child when he slips her hand and darts out towards a busy road, anger can be a sign of love. We shall also look at that glorious paradox as we turn now to the actual texts.

DAVID WINTER

# The divine paradox

The Lord is merciful and gracious, slow to anger and abounding in steadfast love. He will not always accuse, nor will he keep his anger for ever. He does not deal with us according to our sins, nor repay us according to our iniquities. For as the heavens are high above the earth, so great is his steadfast love towards those who fear him; as far as the east is from the west, so far he removes our transgressions from us. As a father has compassion for his children, so the Lord has compassion for those who fear him.

I have chosen this familiar passage from Psalm 103 as the start of these readings simply because it offers a perfect key to the paradox of a loving God who at times exhibits anger. God's anger (or 'wrath') is not temper. He isn't stamping his foot or losing his self-control, as we do when we get angry. His is an anger that is 'compassionate', that cares about the welfare of his children. Did you notice the word *chesedh* twice in these few verses—'steadfast love'? God's very nature doesn't change with mood-swings, as ours does.

The main point the psalmist is making, however, is about the *purpose* of God's anger. Very often, human anger is simply letting off steam or a reaction to a supposed insult, injustice or provocation. God's anger is always and only at sin itself, together with the human folly and disobedience that give rise to it. The old tag about 'hating the sin and loving the sinner' sums it up quite neatly.

When a parent or grandparent corrects a child, even to the point of being angry at the child's wilfulness or disobedience, their motivation is not hatred. It is because we love our children that we want them to have happy, safe, secure lives. The comparison with a father in verse 13 demonstrates the point. It is entirely possible to be compassionate and angry at the same time.

---

*'He removes our transgressions from us' (v. 12). Reflect on what that cost: 'God so loved the world that he gave his only Son' (John 3:16).*

DAVID WINTER

# Cain: envy and anger

Next [Eve] bore [Cain's] brother Abel. Now Abel was a keeper of sheep, and Cain a tiller of the ground. In the course of time Cain brought to the Lord an offering of the fruit of the ground, and Abel for his part brought of the firstlings of his flock, their fat portions. And the Lord had regard for Abel and his offering, but for Cain and his offering he had no regard. So Cain was very angry, and his countenance fell... Cain said to his brother Abel, 'Let us go out to the field.' And when they were in the field, Cain rose up against his brother Abel, and killed him.

The first sin, by Adam and Eve, was to think they knew better than God and to eat the forbidden fruit. The second—perhaps more easily recognisable to us as an evil act—was committed by their son Cain, who killed his brother Abel in a murder motivated by envy. It was the first such, but by no means the last. The precise cause of the attack seems odd to us—something about the relative merits of blood sacrifice and other offerings, perhaps—but the detail in a story from prehistory is not important. Cain's envy was provoked and then overtaken by an uncontrolled anger.

This first homicide, dreadful in its simplicity but also in its premeditation ('Let us go out to the field'), sprang from the powerful toxin of envy. Sin often works in teams: one thing leads to another. Envy seems to be a little sin, but its consequences can be terrible. Sadly, this story in Genesis is of envy associated with worship of the Lord. Whose offering was the better one? Envy and its cousin, jealousy, are not confined to those ancient fields, nor to television studios or city offices. They can also lurk in the choir stalls and the pews. From such miserable roots have sprung jealousy and hatred even within a Christian congregation.

---

*The church litany invites us to pray: 'From envy, hatred and malice, good Lord, deliver us.'*

DAVID WINTER

# Righteous anger

Then Moses turned and went down from the mountain, carrying the two tablets of the covenant in his hands, tablets that were written on both sides, written on the front and on the back... When Joshua heard the noise of the people as they shouted, he said to Moses, 'There is a noise of war in the camp.' But he said, 'It is not the sound made by victors, or the sound made by losers; it is the sound of revellers that I hear.' As soon as he came near the camp and saw the calf and the dancing, Moses' anger burned hot, and he threw the tablets from his hands and broke them at the foot of the mountain. He took the calf that they had made, burned it with fire, ground it to powder, scattered it on the water, and made the Israelites drink it.

Moses had been a very long while up Mount Sinai—so long that the people lost patience. 'We do not know what has become of him,' they said (32:1), and persuaded Aaron that they should make a golden calf to worship, like the other nations around them. This was done, and they celebrated with songs and dancing. Moses and Joshua came down from the mountain, the holy law of God in their hands, to find that the people they had led from Egypt had decided instead to worship a manmade idol.

We already know that Moses had a short fuse. After all, he'd had to flee Egypt after killing a slave-master who was beating a fellow Hebrew (Exodus 2:11–12). Several times the people on their long pilgrimage through the desert had complained about his leadership. Where was the promised food and water? Each time, Moses interceded for them, and food (manna) and water were provided, yet the crowd remained sceptical. Now, in his absence, they had gone too far. 'Moses' anger burned hot' (v. 19). You bet it did! Here, we may feel, was what we call 'righteous anger', a drastic response to a drastic evil.

---

*Our anger is 'righteous' if its concern is God's glory, not ours.*

DAVID WINTER

# Keep calm and carry on

'Take the staff, and assemble the congregation, you and your brother Aaron, and command the rock before their eyes to yield its water. Thus you shall bring water out of the rock for them; thus you shall provide drink for the congregation and their livestock.'... Moses and Aaron gathered the assembly together before the rock, and he said to them, 'Listen, you rebels, shall we bring water for you out of this rock?' Then Moses lifted up his hand and struck the rock twice with his staff; water came out abundantly, and the congregation and their livestock drank. But the Lord said to Moses and Aaron, 'Because you did not trust in me, to show my holiness before the eyes of the Israelites, therefore you shall not bring this assembly into the land that I have given them.'

Moses, as we have seen, always had a problem with anger. In our last reading, we saw his righteous anger at the Israelites' lapse into idolatry. Now we see angry impatience getting the better of him when, for the umpteenth time, they protest about a shortage of water. As usual, he turned to the Lord for help. As usual, that help was both timely and dramatic. God's purpose would be served as Moses and Aaron commanded water to come from the rock face. Surely then the people would realise at last that God was with them on their journey to the promised land?

The sight of the people waiting for a miracle triggered Moses' indignation. His words were angry ('you rebels!') and his action excessive. Instead of speaking in God's name, he struck the rock twice with his staff. The result, from the people's point of view, was satisfactory—plenty of fresh water—but the spiritual message was lost in a fit of pique.

---

*Moses paid a high price for his failure to keep calm and carry out God's command. He would not enter the promised land. Angry words spoken in haste can have unforeseen consequences.*

DAVID WINTER

# Treading the wine press

Then I saw heaven opened, and there was a white horse! Its rider is called Faithful and True, and in righteousness he judges and makes war... He is clothed in a robe dipped in blood, and his name is called The Word of God... From his mouth comes a sharp sword with which to strike down the nations, and he will rule them with a rod of iron; he will tread the wine press of the fury of the wrath of God the Almighty. On his robe and on his thigh he has a name inscribed, 'King of kings and Lord of lords'.

Here we have Revelation's vision of the rider on the white horse. He is clearly identified as Jesus, the 'Word of God' (John 1:1), but this is a very different figure from Revelation's 'Lamb of God' who died to take away the sin of the world. Is it a contradiction or simply another glorious paradox?

The 'sword' that comes from his mouth is the word of God (see Hebrews 4:12 ) that judges the 'nations'. For the purpose of our readings on anger, however, the most vivid part of this awesome vision is that 'he will tread the wine press of the fury of the wrath of God'. What does this mean? Psalm 75:8 speaks of God preparing a cup of 'foaming wine', which 'the wicked of the earth shall drain... to the dregs', and in the garden of Gethsemane Jesus prays about the cup of his Father's will, which he must drink (Matthew 26:39). In John's vision in Revelation 19 he is seen creating that foaming wine as he treads the wine press of God's 'wrath'.

Two different words are used for 'wrath' in Revelation. One carries a sense of profound indignation, the other a strong passion or emotion, something like 'outrage'. Here, uniquely, both are used in the same sentence. What Jesus trod was literally 'the wine of the outrage of the indignation of God'. This is not blind anger or temper, but God's utter indignation at what sin has done to his perfect creation. This is the 'cup' of which Jesus spoke.

---

*The Saviour's trampling feet made the wine. His holy lips drank it for us.*

DAVID WINTER

# Anger and disgust

The Passover of the Jews was near, and Jesus went up to Jerusalem. In the temple he found people selling cattle, sheep, and doves, and the money-changers seated at their tables. Making a whip of cords, he drove all of them out of the temple, both the sheep and the cattle. He also poured out the coins of the money-changers and overturned their tables. He told those who were selling the doves, 'Take these things out of here! Stop making my Father's house a market-place!' His disciples remembered that it was written, 'Zeal for your house will consume me.'

Those of you still puzzling over yesterday's reading may find that today's sheds further light on the subject. All four Gospels record the incident of Jesus 'cleansing the temple', although John places it at the start of the Messiah's ministry rather than the end. The story is the same, however. Jesus entered the holy site and was appalled at its misuse. Everywhere there were traders selling birds and animals for sacrifice, and money-changers translating ordinary currency into the special temple coinage. Business was obviously brisk. Jesus was incensed by the sight of commerce polluting the holy place. His anger was not confined to words, either. Making a whip, he drove the traders out of the temple and tipped over the money-changers' tables. 'Stop making my Father's house a market-place!' he shouted.

There can be no doubt that Jesus was angry (so much for 'Gentle Jesus, meek and mild'!), but, as we have already seen, this was not a 'red mist' kind of anger. His fury was fuelled by disgust. As Mark 11:17 reports, he reminded the crowds that the temple was intended to be 'a house of prayer for all the nations', not 'a den of robbers'. The disciples recognised that his actions were prompted not by hatred of the traders but by 'zeal for God's house'.

*Unless our motives are as pure as the Messiah's, we should probably leave the judging to the one whose judgements are 'pure… and righteous altogether' (Psalm 19:9).*

DAVID WINTER

# Being chastised

'My child, do not regard lightly the discipline of the Lord, or lose heart when you are punished by him; for the Lord disciplines those whom he loves, and chastises every child whom he accepts.' Endure trials for the sake of discipline. God is treating you as children; for what child is there whom a parent does not discipline?... Moreover, we had human parents to discipline us, and we respected them. Should we not be even more willing to be subject to the Father of spirits and live? For they disciplined us for a short time as seemed best to them, but he disciplines us for our good, in order that we may share his holiness. Now, discipline always seems painful rather than pleasant at the time, but later it yields the peaceful fruit of righteousness to those who have been trained by it.

You might question whether chastising ought to be included in a series of readings on 'anger'. It is probably possible to 'chastise' without actually being angry, but the person being chastised usually feels like a victim of anger. 'Put that down at once!' 'Don't be rude to grandma!' 'I'm stopping your pocket money until you learn to say "thank you"!' The chastiser may feel that this is indignation used to good intent, while the one chastised may disagree.

The writer to the Hebrews wanted them to understand that a necessary part of discipleship is discipline, and that sometimes the heavenly Father does exactly what a human one does, rebuking us sharply. The Oxford English Dictionary defines 'to chastise' as 'to reprimand severely'. It's safe to say that being reprimanded severely is seldom a happy experience. The point at issue, however, is not whether it's nice or nasty, but whether its result is a good one.

Human discipline often concerns details of behaviour, good manners and so on. Divine discipline is 'for our good, in order that we may share his holiness' (v. 10). When God reprimands us, it is a sign not of his anger but of his love. That keeps on emerging as a theme in these readings.

---

*'Discipline... yields the peaceful fruit of righteousness' (v. 11).*

DAVID WINTER

# Angry words and their consequences

'You have heard that it was said to those of ancient times, "You shall not murder"; and "whoever murders shall be liable to judgment." But I say to you that if you are angry with a brother or sister, you will be liable to judgment; and if you insult a brother or sister, you will be liable to the council; and if you say, "You fool", you will be liable to the hell of fire. So when you are offering your gift at the altar, if you remember that your brother or sister has something against you, leave your gift there before the altar and go; first be reconciled to your brother or sister, and then come and offer your gift.'

This is the first of six pieces of teaching by Jesus in the Sermon on the Mount about the difference between observing the letter of the law of God and obeying its spirit. Here it's about murder. It's easy to say, 'I haven't murdered anyone, so I've kept the law', but Jesus is concerned with the ways of the human heart. Murder doesn't occur out of a vacuum, but has its roots in much more day-to-day failures, the foremost of which is anger—or, more specifically here, angry words. So anyone who is angry with a 'brother or sister' (in context, a fellow disciple) will be 'judged', and so will anyone who 'insults' them or calls them a 'fool'. This may seem a bit extreme, but compare it with the similar remarks of Jesus about adultery and you will see what he is driving at (5:27–28). Serious sin often has apparently harmless roots.

Jesus loved to use the figure of speech called hyperbole—deliberately exaggerating to make his point more forcefully. He himself called the religious hypocrites 'blind fools' (Matthew 23:17), so we should not take this language too literally, but what we should do is take to heart its warning. Angry words often—too often—lead to angry, cruel and even violent actions.

---

*Sticks and stones may break our bones, but words can cause lifelong wounds.*

DAVID WINTER

# Taming the tongue

How great a forest is set ablaze by a small fire! And the tongue is a fire. The tongue is placed among our members as a world of iniquity; it stains the whole body, sets on fire the cycle of nature, and is itself set on fire by hell. For every species of beast and bird, of reptile and sea creature, can be tamed and has been tamed by the human species, but no one can tame the tongue—a restless evil, full of deadly poison. With it we bless the Lord and Father, and with it we curse those who are made in the likeness of God. From the same mouth come blessing and cursing. My brothers and sisters, this ought not to be so.

If this letter, as long tradition suggests, has its origins in the teaching of James the brother of Jesus (Galatians 1:19), presumably he would have been present at the Sermon on the Mount. Perhaps he felt that the Christians he was addressing in the church of the apostolic era needed some practical help and advice in fulfilling the exhortations of his brother. Whether that is so or not, this passage picks up the same topic as yesterday's reading, with a series of robust warnings about the moral perils of the unfettered tongue.

It's hard to deny his main point, that the tongue (speech) has set fire to many human bonfires. Not only in the matter of warfare between nations, but in ordinary daily life, angry words are cheap and common but sometimes devastating in their consequences. Angry speech does indeed seem to be set alight by the fire of hell (*gehenna*: James is using a word favoured by Jesus to describe judgement). There is, as James observes, an appalling contradiction between singing God's praises and then using the same mouth and lips to curse, ridicule or abuse those made in his image. 'This ought not to be so.'

---

*'Set a guard over my mouth, O Lord; keep watch over the door of my lips' (Psalm 141:3).*

DAVID WINTER

# Some practical advice

You were taught to put away your former way of life, your old self, corrupt and deluded by its lusts, and to be renewed in the spirit of your minds, and to clothe yourselves with the new self, created according to the likeness of God in true righteousness and holiness. So then, putting away falsehood, let all of us speak the truth to our neighbours, for we are members of one another. Be angry but do not sin; do not let the sun go down on your anger, and do not make room for the devil.

In our last two readings, Jesus and James, in their very contrasting ways, have made clear the danger of the consequences of anger. Now we have the apostle Paul, in a more pastoral way, trying to help the Christians at Ephesus to abandon their former way of life and to live the new life in Christ that they have embraced. In a favourite phrase of his, this will involve 'putting away' some unhelpful things. He identifies two—falsehood (that is, not speaking the truth) and anger. His advice about anger occupies only 24 words, but many of us have found them enormously and practically helpful.

'Be angry,' he says, somewhat surprisingly. That's not an encouragement to do it, of course, but a recognition that, as fallen humans, we will from time to time be angry. (Paul himself was certainly capable of the odd explosion!) 'Be angry', but don't let it become a sin. Control your anger, he tells them, and then gives a splendid piece of practical advice: 'do not let the sun go down on your anger'. In fact, Paul uses a different word here for 'anger', one that implies provocation. Don't let the argument rumble on and get worse, he means. As Jesus said in his comments, be 'reconciled' to your brother or sister (Matthew 5:24). It's a simple, biblical and effective control mechanism: make up before bedtime!

---

*When we are angry, it's usually with a person rather than a thing. That means that two people are involved. 'A soft answer turns away wrath' (Proverbs 15:1).*

DAVID WINTER

# Being a peacemaker

'Blessed are the peacemakers, for they will be called children of God. Blessed are those who are persecuted for righteousness' sake, for theirs is the kingdom of heaven. Blessed are you when people revile you and persecute you and utter all kinds of evil against you falsely on my account. Rejoice and be glad, for your reward is great in heaven, for in the same way they persecuted the prophets who were before you. You are the salt of the earth; but if salt has lost its taste, how can its saltiness be restored?'

The Beatitudes, as they are called, are very familiar, of course: they list all the characteristics that, according to Jesus, make for a happy, 'blessed' life. The last few, however, introduce what seems to be a different note. Having been told that the 'peacemakers' are blessed, we are then invited to consider what living at peace in a sinful world might actually involve. How is it 'blessed' to be falsely accused, abused and reviled in the name of Jesus? And how can we be 'peacemakers' in that kind of situation?

The next words begin Jesus' answer to those questions. Christians —the 'people of the kingdom'—are the 'salt of the earth' and the 'light of the world' (see 5:14). Salt, in the ancient world, was the universal means of countering corruption and decay. Light is the universal enemy of darkness. Christ's people are present in the world to hold back the continuing consequences of the fall—corruption and evil—and they are, more positively, to reflect the light of Jesus (who is himself 'the light of the world', John 8:12) into its darkest places. Far from countering evil with evil, insult with insult, blow with blow, we are to be his peacemakers. We turn the other cheek, give away our overcoats and go the second mile (5:39–41). Jesus never said it would be easy to follow him.

To be salt and light is a high calling—and peacemakers are happy people.

---

*Jesus 'made peace through the blood of his cross' (Colossians 1:20). Peacemaking can be a costly business.*

DAVID WINTER

# Anger, compassion and steadfast love

Will the Lord spurn for ever, and never again be favourable? Has his steadfast love ceased for ever? Are his promises at an end for all time? Has God forgotten to be gracious? Has he in anger shut up his compassion? And I say, 'It is my grief that the right hand of the Most High has changed.' I will call to mind the deeds of the Lord; I will remember your wonders of old. I will meditate on all your work, and muse on your mighty deeds. Your way, O God, is holy. What god is so great as our God?

This is one of many psalms in which the writer opens with a very candid expression of his doubts ('grief' is an interesting word in verse 10) about whether God is as 'steadfast' in his love as he is reputed to be. Could it even be that his 'right hand' (his saving power) 'has changed'?

'Steadfast love', as we've noted already, is one of the most frequently used phrases in the Hebrew scriptures to describe God's most precious gift to us. The King James Version translates it rather beautifully as 'loving-kindness'. However, 'in the day of my trouble' (77:2), unable to get to sleep at night (77:4), the psalmist begins to fret. Could it be that God's anger at our sins has 'shut up his compassion'? What a terrible thought!

However, as almost always in the Psalter, there is a happy ending. Of course God's steadfast love is still true. When the night-time doubts are reviewed in the light of dawn, and especially when we consider God's deeds in the past, the 'wonders of old' and the holiness of his ways with us now, only one conclusion can be drawn. He is what he has always been. Our God is great, and steadfast to the end.

---

*Doubt is not a sin; unbelief is. When days are dark and troubles come, we may momentarily be anxious that the God who holds us in his love has changed. In fact, it is we who change with circumstances. With our heavenly Father there is 'no variation or shadow due to change' (James 1:17).*

DAVID WINTER

# Practical advice

The evil are ensnared by the transgression of their lips, but the righteous escape from trouble… Fools think their own way is right, but the wise listen to advice. Fools show their anger at once, but the prudent ignore an insult. Whoever speaks the truth gives honest evidence, but a false witness speaks deceitfully. Rash words are like sword thrusts, but the tongue of the wise brings healing. Truthful lips endure forever, but a lying tongue lasts only a moment.

The book of Proverbs offers exactly what its title implies—brief, punchy, wise sayings. They don't follow any plan or scheme: one saying pops up, and then another. But I've chosen here a short sequence of sayings which relate to issues that have surfaced in many of our readings on anger—the connection of the words we speak with the anger we feel. Jesus and James, in their different ways, noted that connection, and both warned about the 'transgression of the lips'.

The contrasts here are built up cleverly. The fool ignores advice, but the wise listens to it. The impetuous are too quick to reveal their inner anger, whereas the prudent ignore provocation. The honest witness speaks the truth, while the deceitfulness of the false witness spreads confusion. Rash words are like sword thrusts (what a vivid image!), whereas wise words have healing properties. The truth is ultimately eternal; lies are soon revealed for what they are.

The book of Proverbs has a kind of repetitive chorus: 'The fear of the Lord is the beginning of wisdom' (Proverbs 1:7 and four more occasions). Although these sayings may, at first sight, seem to have no more authority than any of the ordinary proverbs we have known since childhood, the clue is in that chorus. Those who respect God and want to please him will address the issues raised by the sayings themselves. In doing so, they will find not only 'wisdom' but a way of living peaceably with their family, friends and neighbours.

---

*'The tongue of the wise brings healing' from the painful 'sword thrusts' of anger.*

DAVID WINTER

# Giving and getting a blessing

Finally, all of you, have unity of spirit, sympathy, love for one another, a tender heart, and a humble mind. Do not repay evil for evil or abuse for abuse; but, on the contrary, repay with a blessing. It is for this that you were called—that you might inherit a blessing. For 'Those who desire life and desire to see good days, let them keep their tongues from evil and their lips from speaking deceit; let them turn away from evil and do good; let them seek peace and pursue it.'

Here is an apostolic 'last word'. 'Finally', when you've done everything else, attend to these issues and you will be a blessing to your neighbours and receive God's blessing yourself. The issues are precisely those we have been reading about over the last fortnight—avoiding confrontation, ignoring abuse and overcoming evil with good. Instead of emphasising the problems, the writer simply concentrates on the positives—unity of spirit, sympathy, love for one another, tender hearts and humble minds. It is, as they say nowadays, a challenging agenda.

Once again, as we saw in Proverbs, there are contrasts to note. Don't keep a score of wrongs; don't repay evil with evil; don't abuse those who abuse you. On the contrary, repay all those ugly and angry things with a blessing. It reflects the words of Jesus, 'Pray for those who persecute you' (Matthew 5:44). There are also further specific warnings, of course: keep your tongue from evil and your lips from deceit. Turn away from evil. But the positive is part of the total package: do good, seek peace and pursue it. In other words, don't just hope or simply pray for peace, but pursue a way of life that creates it. In the words of Jesus, be a 'peacemaker'.

---

*In the end, anger and hatred will be defeated only by their essential opposites, peace and love—which are precisely the gifts that God gives to those who turn angry words into prayers of blessing.*

DAVID WINTER

# Easter with Matthew

I am writing this just days after celebrating Christmas, and in one sense it feels strange to have jumped ahead from the manger to the cross, from the news of a Saviour's birth to the events of Holy Week and Easter. Yet, as I sat in a carol service just before Christmas, there was a cross on the Communion table in my direct line of sight. The Gospel reading for Christmas Day, John 1, implies a battle between life and death that is played out in the events of Holy Week and Easter. 'The light shines in the darkness, and the darkness did not overcome it' (John 1:5) and 'To all who received him, who believed in his name, he gave power to become children of God' (v. 12). Incarnation and redemption are inextricably linked. The late bishop of Winchester, J.V. Taylor, put it most vividly in his poem 'Diptych': 'He who lay curled in Mary's womb, starting and ending in a cave, has broken new-born from the tomb.'

'Who is this?' is the question that comes again and again as we contemplate Jesus. He is Immanuel, God-with-us, but what kind of God? Christian doctrine holds together the divinity and humanity of Jesus, and we can only understand the events of Holy Week and Easter in the light of both. Only as God could he redeem us, but only as a human being could he identify fully with us. The events of Holy Week and Easter reveal God to us most fully, as he is in Jesus. Crucified, dead and buried, he rose again, and in his resurrection body he bears the scars of his suffering, borne on our behalf. On Easter Day we reach the glorious climax of the Easter story. As post-Easter people, we are called to life even in the face of death, because Jesus is fully alive. This is the good news we have to share with a broken and disillusioned world. 'In him was life, and the life was the light of all people' (John 1:4). As we are 'in Christ', may we be drawn again to the source of our life and so choose life each day.

LIZ HOARE

# True majesty

[The disciples] brought the donkey and the colt, and put their cloaks on them, and he sat on them. A very large crowd spread their cloaks on the road, and others cut branches from the trees and spread them on the road. The crowds that went ahead of him and that followed were shouting, 'Hosanna to the Son of David!'

So begins the journey to Jerusalem, where Jesus will fulfil his destiny. Palm Sunday, the beginning of what we call Holy Week, is a joyous occasion, tinged with foreboding. The sense of fulfilment, of history at a turning point, is overwhelming in Matthew's Gospel, as the entry into Jerusalem recalls two Old Testament passages, Zechariah 9:9 and Isaiah 62:11, both of which refer to the coming of a saviour.

The figure in Zechariah is humble and peaceful, in contrast to the popular idea of the Messiah as a military victor. The word 'humble' used by Zechariah has the same meaning as 'gentle' in Matthew 11:29 and 'meek' in Matthew 5:5, and the donkey emphasises the peaceful nature of Jesus' coming. This Messiah's destiny leads to suffering and humiliation, not victory and triumph through force. We humans seem destined to believe that only the use of force will achieve what we think is right, and we assume that leadership must be associated with all the trappings of power (which is why the wise men went first to King Herod's court in their search for Jesus: Matthew 2:1–2).

The irony of the situation in this scene is vivid. The crowd who gather to shout 'Hosanna' are full of joy and expectation. The cloaks spread underfoot, the waving of palm branches and shouts of acclamation to 'the Son of David' all point to the understanding that Jesus is the long-awaited deliverer who will free them from their oppressors and turn their fortunes around. Jesus was indeed the long-expected deliverer and the answer to all their, and our, prayers and longings, but they and we have to learn to let God do things his way rather than ours. The obvious quick-fix is not the path to spiritual insight and maturity.

---

*Father, save me from the mistaken belief that your kingdom will come by displays of power. Amen*

LIZ HOARE

# Who is Jesus?

Now while the Pharisees were gathered together, Jesus asked them this question: 'What do you think of the Messiah? Whose son is he?' They said to him, 'The son of David.' He said to them, 'How is it then that David by the Spirit calls him Lord, saying, "The Lord said to my Lord, 'Sit at my right hand, until I put your enemies under your feet'"? If David thus calls him Lord, how can he be his son?'

Many of us will have felt caught out by clever questions from religious sceptics. The Pharisees have made a number of attempts to trap Jesus with their clever conundrums but here Jesus turns the tables and puts a question to them. As in yesterday's reading, the question is about his identity: 'Is the Messiah David's son or David's Lord?' The Pharisees were the experts when it came to the identity of the Messiah; they knew the answer to the first question straight away. It was the second question that tied them in knots. Everyone knew that a father did not humble himself before his offspring, to call him 'Lord'. It was the other way round. The saddest part of this scene, of course, is that the answer to the question was standing in front of them, literally in the flesh.

The fact that the Messiah is both David's son and David's Lord is a mystery, but the gospel is the mystery of God made known in the person of Jesus. As the arrest, trial and crucifixion will demonstrate, Jesus really is David's son, the true king of Israel, and also David's Lord—and not only David's but Lord of all that is.

Jesus' question is not an academic question for scholars only; this is the question that confronts all of us in Jesus' own person. As we follow his journey to the cross in the Gospel of Matthew (who also wants us to know who Jesus is), we will discover that Jesus is 'descended from David according to the flesh' but is also 'Son of God with power' (Romans 1:3–4).

---

*Jesus, Lord and Master, help me to see you more clearly, love you more dearly and follow you more nearly, day by day. Amen*

LIZ HOARE

# Such love

Now while Jesus was at Bethany in the house of Simon the leper, a woman came to him with an alabaster jar of very costly ointment, and she poured it on his head as he sat at the table. But when the disciples saw it, they were angry and said, 'Why this waste? For this ointment could have been sold for a large sum, and the money given to the poor.' But Jesus, aware of this, said to them, 'Why do you trouble the woman? She has performed a good service for me. For you always have the poor with you, but you will not always have me. By pouring this ointment on my body she has prepared me for burial.'

Imagine the scene at Simon's house. How would you have felt to witness the woman's actions? What would you have thought? Does it make any difference to recall that, a little earlier, Jesus had told his disciples that the Son of Man would be handed over to be crucified (26:2)? Matthew also tells us that the chief priests and elders were plotting together to arrest and kill Jesus (26:4).

Jesus interprets the woman's seemingly pointless extravagance as a beautiful act, full of symbolic meaning. By pouring the costly ointment from the jar (which she would have had to break to get the contents out), she was expressing her overflowing love for him. Such effusive love could make us feel very uncomfortable; it certainly made the disciples angry, but look at Jesus' reaction. He welcomed the woman's gesture and linked it for ever with the gospel by saying, 'Wherever this good news is proclaimed in the whole world, what she has done will be told in remembrance of her' (26:13).

In the midst of mounting tension and impending violence, here is a gentle moment when Jesus recognises and acknowledges a woman's action. He accepts her devotion and honours her in return. Has your love for Jesus ever led you to do something out of the ordinary, or something that risked being misinterpreted?

---

*'My song is love unknown, my Saviour's love to me, love to the loveless shown, that they might lovely be. This is my friend, in whose sweet praise I all my days could gladly spend' (Henry Crossman).*

LIZ HOARE

# He laid down his life for his friends

Then one of the twelve, who was called Judas Iscariot, went to the chief priests and said, 'What will you give me if I betray him to you?' They paid him thirty pieces of silver. And from that moment he began to look for an opportunity to betray him. On the first day of Unleavened Bread the disciples came to Jesus, saying, 'Where do you want us to make the preparations for you to eat the Passover?' He said, 'Go into the city to a certain man, and say to him, "The Teacher says, My time is near; I will keep the Passover at your house with my disciples."'

The tension mounts as Judas takes the fateful step of offering to betray his master. Meanwhile, Jesus, as a devout Jew, focuses on making arrangements to keep the Passover. The contrast between the deluded nature of Judas and the clarity and purpose of Jesus is clearly marked by Matthew. However, he gives us no indication of Judas's reasons for turning traitor: we will probably never understand them.

Jesus has a clear idea about the significance of the Passover for his own destiny. Matthew presents him as the Son of Man who will give his life for the world. At the time of the first Passover, Moses told the Israelites to mark the lintels of their doors with the blood of the slaughtered lambs so that the angel of God would 'pass over' them to deliver them (Exodus 12:1–13). Jesus, the lamb of God 'slaughtered from the foundation of the world' (Revelation 13:8), will be handed over and betrayed by one of his own—so fulfilling the scriptures that foretold how it would happen (Matthew 26:24, 54, 56).

Before that happens, though, he first sits down with his disciples, including Judas, to share a meal. You may like to read further in Matthew 26 (vv. 26–29) to see how Jesus turned the meal around to point to himself, identifying the bread and wine with his own body and blood, offered up for Peter, James and John, Judas, me and you.

---

*Thank you, Lord Jesus, for the single-minded sense of purpose that took you to the cross, to shed your blood for me.*

LIZ HOARE

# The agony of the cross

Then Jesus went with them to a place called Gethsemane; and he said to his disciples, 'Sit here while I go over there and pray.' He took with him Peter and the two sons of Zebedee, and began to be grieved and agitated. Then he said to them, 'I am deeply grieved, even to death; remain here, and stay awake with me.' And going a little farther, he threw himself on the ground and prayed, 'My Father, if it is possible, let this cup pass from me; yet not what I want but what you want.'

Here in Gethsemane we are given a glimpse of the cost of Jesus' journey to the cross. Gethsemane means 'olive press' and this helps us picture the crushing anguish that Jesus was preparing himself to face. It also recalls Old Testament passages such as Isaiah 63:3, which pictures the treading of grapes in a wine press, thus linking Israel's story to Jesus.

We are told that Jesus 'began to be grieved and agitated' (v. 37). His words to his disciples about his grief (v. 38) allude to Psalm 42:6 and 43:5, which speak of a soul that is 'cast down', and the addition of the words 'even to death' show the depth of anguish he was feeling. He could see before him the cup that he was being asked to drink, and he struggled with the implications.

The image of the cup (v. 39) is multifaceted. Jesus had just taken a cup of wine at the Passover, blessed it and explained it as his blood 'poured out for many for the forgiveness of sins' (26:27–28). The cup is also an Old Testament metaphor for punishment and retribution, and here it involves suffering and death as well.

Was there no other way? Perhaps Jesus knew there was not, and he was not trying to sidestep his destiny, but he shrank from it nevertheless. Would it have made any difference if his disciples had stayed awake? We might sometimes feel that to say 'Your will be done' is a cop-out in prayer, but Jesus was praying the same prayer he had taught his disciples (Matthew 6:10), which we too take as our model.

---

*Are you being asked to 'stay awake and pray' on someone's behalf? Is 'Your will be done' the right way to pray in your circumstances today?*

LIZ HOARE

# And darkness fell

From noon on, darkness came over the whole land until three in the afternoon. And about three o'clock Jesus cried with a loud voice, 'Eli, Eli, lema sabachthani?' that is, 'My God, my God, why have you forsaken me?' When some of the bystanders heard it, they said, 'This man is calling for Elijah.' At once one of them ran and got a sponge, filled it with sour wine, put it on a stick, and gave it to him to drink. But the others said, 'Wait, let us see whether Elijah will come to save him.' Then Jesus cried again with a loud voice and breathed his last. At that moment the curtain of the temple was torn in two, from top to bottom. The earth shook, and the rocks were split.

In Matthew's Gospel, the words known as 'the cry of dereliction' are the only ones that Jesus is recorded to have uttered from the cross. So vivid were they that the original language of Aramaic was imprinted on the bystanders' memories. When someone approaches the moment of death, they withdraw into a place alone, but the sense of abandonment that Jesus expresses here is of a different order altogether. We cannot soften the dereliction by claiming that God was with him in the darkness, for his own cry of forsakenness contradicts us. As he hung on the cross, the weight of sin and evil was such that he was cut off completely from his heavenly Father and experienced total abandonment.

The fact that this was necessary for the cross to achieve its work does not lessen the intensity of Jesus' feelings, but it does demonstrate the depth of God's love for the world. Many people, encountering extreme suffering or despair, have been helped by the knowledge that Jesus experienced such abandonment, even though it may not answer the question 'Why?' In the ancient Anglo-Saxon poem 'The Dream of the Rood' (rood meaning 'cross'), the cross narrates the story and, as Jesus dies, relates how the entire creation reels at this blackest of moments in history. Matthew notes that the earth shook and the temple curtain was torn from top to bottom (v. 51).

---

*Jesus was cut off from the Father so that we could freely enter his presence.*

LIZ HOARE

# Watching and waiting

When it was evening, there came a rich man from Arimathea, named Joseph, who was also a disciple of Jesus. He went to Pilate and asked for the body of Jesus; then Pilate ordered it to be given to him. So Joseph took the body and wrapped it in a clean linen cloth and laid it in his own new tomb, which he had hewn in the rock. He then rolled a great stone to the door of the tomb and went away. Mary Magdalene and the other Mary were there, sitting opposite the tomb.

In many ways, the situation following the crucifixion was even more dark and hopeless than the events of Good Friday. On this day Jesus lay in the grave and there was nothing left for his followers to hope for. The finality of rolling the stone across the entrance must have been crushing to those who witnessed it. Yet the two Marys were there keeping watch, waiting until they could return with spices to tend to the body of their teacher.

Most of us struggle with Holy Saturday and all that it represents. For the bereaved, the period of time between the death of a loved one and the funeral can feel like living in suspended animation, everything on hold and a physical weight of darkness all around. We want it to end, just as, in the story of Jesus' death, we want to hurry on to Easter Day and the joyful denouement of resurrection.

Resurrection will come, but first we need to grasp the truth that Jesus shared not only our life on earth but also our death. Every one of us has to die, and Jesus himself has experienced what it is like—but that is not all. In sharing our death, he has transformed it because of who he is.

The service of Compline in the Book of Common Prayer includes a prayer that begins: 'O Lord Jesus Christ, Son of the living God, who at this evening hour didst rest in the sepulchre, and didst thereby sanctify the grave to be a bed of hope to Thy people…'

---

*Reflect on these words as you watch and wait today.*

LIZ HOARE

# He is risen!

After the sabbath, as the first day of the week was dawning, Mary Magdalene and the other Mary went to see the tomb. And suddenly there was a great earthquake; for an angel of the Lord, descending from heaven, came and rolled back the stone and sat on it. His appearance was like lightning, and his clothing white as snow. For fear of him the guards shook and became like dead men. But the angel said to the women, 'Do not be afraid; I know that you are looking for Jesus who was crucified. He is not here; for he has been raised, as he said. Come, see the place where he lay.'

Another earthquake and more dramatic scenes, but this time heralding good news. In the Church of the Holy Sepulchre in Jerusalem, at the reputed site where Jesus was buried, the words 'He is not here; he is risen' are inscribed in stone. Every pilgrim who bends low to see the place where Jesus lay is reminded that we worship a risen Lord. So the angel invited the women to look and see that he was not there any longer.

The resurrection is the climax of Matthew's Gospel and transforms everything he has written so far. Matthew wants his readers to understand not only what Jesus said and did, but also who he was, in the light of the resurrection. The resurrection of Jesus changes everything that went before it. It makes us understand Jesus' words and deeds in a totally new way.

The dramatic events aside, life went on as before: the Romans were still in power, the poor remained poor and the religious leaders did not want to know. But for those who saw and believed, it slowly dawned, like the emergence of a new day (v. 1), that Jesus was alive. Easter celebrates the victory of life over death, a struggle that goes on around us every day. Jesus said, 'I am the resurrection and the life' (John 11:25). His life is ongoing, and it transforms every dead situation. 'Because I live, you also will live' (John 14:19).

---

*Lord, transform all my days with your life-giving Spirit. Amen*

LIZ HOARE

# Transforming presence

[The angel said] 'Then go quickly and tell his disciples, "He has been raised from the dead, and indeed he is going ahead of you to Galilee; there you will see him." This is my message for you.' So they left the tomb quickly with fear and great joy, and ran to tell his disciples. Suddenly Jesus met them and said, 'Greetings!' And they came to him, took hold of his feet, and worshipped him. Then Jesus said to them, 'Do not be afraid; go and tell my brothers to go to Galilee; there they will see me.'

The mixture of fear and joy mentioned in verse 8 is very true to life. The women must have hardly dared to believe. As we saw yesterday, their understanding grew slowly, like the dawning of the day. They may have wondered, but they could not keep the good news to themselves, so they did as the angel told them and went to tell the other disciples.

J.V. Taylor points out the significance of being met by Jesus in Galilee as opposed to Jerusalem. The latter symbolises the safe stronghold of faith, where worship is offered—and indeed God does meet us there. Galilee, however, is the world at large, the secular world of work, where people are not interested in God or religion and their values do not reflect the gospel. Yet, this is where Jesus promises to meet us, as his message to the disciples indicates. This is where we will discover his life, his power and transforming presence.

'Galilee' is also where the challenge of following the risen Christ will confront each one of us and invite us to be part of the transformation he is determined to bring about in the world. It will be costly and will require courage, but this is where the reality of the resurrection will set us free to live his way. Taylor notes that Galilee by no means replaces Jerusalem, for it is in Jerusalem, the place of worship, that we are strengthened by reaffirming and re-enacting the fundamentals of our faith in the risen Lord.

---

*'Lord Jesus Christ, alive and at large in the world, help me to follow and find you there today, in the places where I work, meet people, spend money and make plans' (J.V. Taylor).*

LIZ HOARE

# Learning to trust

Now the eleven disciples went to Galilee, to the mountain to which Jesus had directed them. When they saw him, they worshipped him; but some doubted. And Jesus came and said to them, 'All authority in heaven and on earth has been given to me. Go therefore and make disciples of all nations, baptising them in the name of the Father and of the Son and of the Holy Spirit, and teaching them to obey everything that I have commanded you. And remember, I am with you always, to the end of the age.'

Does verse 17 mean that some doubted although they all worshipped him, or that some worshipped and some, who doubted, did not? If some people doubted even with the risen Jesus standing before them, what hope have we today, who have to walk by faith and not by sight? What place has doubt in the life of faith?

If you struggle with the question of whether Jesus really did rise from the dead, the best way forward may be to keep company with other believers. Jesus has promised to be with his followers: 'I am with you' are four simple words that carry a weight of meaning and will bear the heaviest burden of doubt. They send us back to Sinai and Moses' encounter with God in the burning bush, the God who revealed himself as 'I am'. Here is Jesus claiming all authority, commanding his disciples to baptise others 'in the name of the Father and of the Son and of the Holy Spirit'.

The original Greek puts these four words in a different order, so they read 'I-with you-am'. It's as if we are drawn right into the life of the Trinity—the Father, the Son and the Holy Spirit—and are held there securely with all our doubts, all our searching, and all our struggles to obey. Did the doubters think that the command to 'make disciples' did not apply to them, because of their doubts? Our faltering witness may sound so much less articulate than we would like, but Jesus is with us to all eternity. If we can say that, we have something worth saying.

---

*O Lord, may the sense of your presence today overcome my fears and doubts. Please help my unbelief. Amen*

LIZ HOARE

# Not in vain

When this perishable body puts on imperishability, and this mortal body puts on immortality, then the saying that is written will be fulfilled: 'Death has been swallowed up in victory.' 'Where, O death, is your victory? Where, O death, is your sting?' The sting of death is sin, and the power of sin is the law. But thanks be to God, who gives us the victory through our Lord Jesus Christ. Therefore, my beloved, be steadfast, immovable, always excelling in the work of the Lord, because you know that in the Lord your labour is not in vain.

Faith in the resurrection implies a new vision of human destiny. It is not saying that nobody need die a physical death any more; that is patently not the case. Here Paul is talking about the moment when we will know that death itself has been defeated. The promise of our future resurrection does not make death irrelevant or of no account. Death affects all of us, Christians as well as everyone else. We grieve for our loved ones who have died and we cannot guarantee an easy death for ourselves. Death remains an enemy (1 Corinthians 15:26), and to pretend otherwise is to diminish the power of the resurrection.

What Paul is doing here is pointing us in triumph to our future hope and urging us to make sure that we live differently now in the light of that hope. Knowing that death is a defeated enemy, we may still grieve, but we can also live in hope that finds expression in the way we live. We live in between the resurrection of Jesus and the final resurrection at the end of this age, and there is work to be done. This work is not in vain (v. 58), so we must attend to it steadfastly, without distraction and with absolute commitment. We are not simply biding our time, hanging around waiting. We are participating in God's purposes for the world. On their completion, everything that is of God will be included there, complete and whole.

---

*Lord Jesus, help me to see my life in the light of the kingdom and to work towards that kingdom, confident that my work is not in vain. Amen*

LIZ HOARE

# Growing in Christ

Therefore, since we are justified by faith, we have peace with God through our Lord Jesus Christ. Through him we have obtained access to this grace in which we stand, and we rejoice in our hope of sharing the glory of God. More than that, we rejoice in our sufferings, knowing that suffering produces endurance, and endurance produces character, and character produces hope, and hope does not disappoint us, because God's love has been poured into our hearts through the Holy Spirit which has been given to us.

The knowledge that we have peace with God because we have been justified by faith is the gift of the risen Christ, freely given to us. It sets us free from the past that binds and it enables us to look forward in hope to sharing God's life for ever. We are set free for the future because the cross has set us free from the past. But what are we to do in the meantime, and why is there still so much suffering in the world, that afflicts Christians and others alike?

Looking to the future means that we can rejoice in our hope of the glory of God (v. 2), and it means that we can even rejoice in suffering (v. 3). Paul is not saying here that we should go looking for suffering, or that the hope of glory in the future enables us to endure affliction in the present. Suffering keeps us from trusting in ourselves, for our hope rests entirely on what God has done for us in Christ.

We live in the in-between times, and Paul says that we are called to develop Christian character. It is God's love for us, rather than our love for him, that makes us confident of our hope. That love is the basis for our knowledge that we have peace with God (v. 1). Peace is what we experience when we know that we are loved. We might agree with the person who has said that 'peace is love resting'.

---

*Lord Jesus, may my hope rest in your peace and your love today. Amen*

LIZ HOARE

# The world made whole

The creation itself will be set free from its bondage to decay and will obtain the freedom of the glory of the children of God. We know that the whole creation has been groaning in labour pains until now; and not only the creation, but we ourselves, who have the first fruits of the Spirit, groan inwardly while we wait for adoption, the redemption of our bodies. For in hope we were saved. Now hope that is seen is not hope. For who hopes for what is seen? But if we hope for what we do not see, we wait for it with patience.

Matthew's Gospel records the impact of Jesus' death and resurrection on the created world—shown in two earthquakes (Matthew 27:51; 28:2). Just as the full implications of the truth that Jesus rose from the dead still await human beings, so Paul writes here of the groaning of creation as it awaits its full redemption. This fact that creation 'groans' confronts us everywhere—not only in the suffering of humanity but also in the decay and destruction of the created world. Our growing awareness of the link between human values and vision and their impact on our planet demonstrates that there are spiritual issues involved. The restoration of human beings to be what God originally intended will involve restoring creation to its proper place, so that we can live in harmony with it.

The 'first fruits' of the harvest in Paul's time were full of the promise that the rest of the harvest was on its way and would eventually be gathered in. The barns were not yet full, but there was joy in anticipating that they would be full, in time. Paul and the first Christians put their trust in the resurrection of Jesus, believing that they too, along with all Christians and the whole of creation, would one day experience resurrection.

Romans 8 makes a clear link between the resurrection of human beings and the healing of the physical universe. Care for God's creation is an essential dimension of Christian discipleship and mission, so that we keep in step with God's intentions for his world.

---

*Ask God how you and your church could play your part in working towards 'the freedom of the glory of the children of God'.*

LIZ HOARE

# Everything we need for salvation

Who will bring any charge against God's elect? It is God who justifies. Who is to condemn? It is Christ Jesus, who died, yes, who was raised, who is at the right hand of God, who indeed intercedes for us. Who will separate us from the love of Christ? Will hardship, or distress, or persecution, or famine, or nakedness, or peril, or sword?... No, in all these things we are more than conquerors through him who loved us. I am convinced that neither death, nor life, nor angels, nor rulers, nor things present, nor things to come, nor powers, nor height, nor depth, nor anything else in all creation, will be able to separate us from the love of God in Christ Jesus our Lord.

To know that someone is praying for us is a great strength and comfort. They may not know how to pray, but simply bringing us to the feet of the risen Lord is enough. Here Paul states that Jesus is risen and alive and has taken his place at the right hand of God, and that he now prays for us to the Father. We are brought by name into the fellowship of the holy Trinity, where we are known and loved (see also 1 John 2:1; Hebrews 7:25). The fact that God is for us, that he loves us, is proved by the life, death and resurrection of Jesus Christ. Jesus stands as the pledge that God will give us every good thing (Romans 8:32), or everything we need for salvation. We have nothing to fear.

To reinforce his point, Paul uses a rhetorical question, listing a host of perils that might seem threatening to a believer's security in Christ. Life may be full of insecurities both now and in the unknown future, but we need not fear. Not even death itself, or the unseen powers of the universe, can overcome the power of God's love for us which is in Jesus Christ our Lord (v. 39).

---

*Spend some time bringing to the Lord the things that you most fear, which threaten your sense of his presence with you.*

LIZ HOARE

# Cairns

A journey through the Bible is like a twisting pathway, winding its way through landscapes both familiar and unknown, sometimes terrifying, at other times filled with love and reassurance. We are encouraged, exhorted, berated, loved and taught in turns as we journey through the different books that tell the story of our faith.

At intervals along this pathway we read about mounds of stones, or cairns. Cairns are human-made piles of stones, used as signs or markers. They can vary in size from the very small to those that tower overhead, but each one of them is built with a purpose. Some of these stones have been erected as memorials to those who have been loved. So, in the Old Testament, Jacob builds a huge memorial to his beloved Rachel when she dies giving birth to Benjamin (Genesis 35:16–20). Some are built as warnings against treachery, like the pile of stones used to bury Achan after he had been stoned to death for stealing (Joshua 7:25–26). Others are used to communicate more directly with those who follow after.

In the following notes, we will be looking at the different ways in which these simple heaps of stones have been used. They are reminders of tremendous acts of bravery, monuments to God's promises, places where the story of God's faithfulness can be told and retold to successive generations. These stones act as signposts or waymarks, helping us to take the correct path. They contain the wisdom of those who have gone before us, the dreams of those who helped to shape the faith of their people, the vision for a future as God's children. Best of all, when we come to look at the role of these humble objects in the New Testament, we will see how these stones, these signs, take on flesh and blood as Jesus becomes the cornerstone of our faith, the foundation stone of the kingdom.

Finally, we too will be invited not simply to walk past but to become living stones ourselves, signs to others of the journey of faith and the hope that leads to new life. We are invited not because of our own goodness but through God's grace, invited to become part of the story through the redeeming sacrifice of Christ, built up by his love into a living temple.

SALLY WELCH

# A sign of commitment

So Jacob rose early in the morning, and he took the stone that he had put under his head and set it up for a pillar and poured oil on the top of it. He called that place Bethel; but the name of the city was Luz at the first. Then Jacob made a vow, saying, 'If God will be with me, and will keep me in this way that I go, and will give me bread to eat and clothing to wear, so that I come again to my father's house in peace, then the Lord shall be my God, and this stone, which I have set up for a pillar, shall be God's house; and of all that you give me I will surely give one-tenth to you.'

Jacob is leaving the land of his birth to look for a wife and to make his way in the world. Falling asleep for the night, he has a strange dream of angels ascending and descending a ladder, and of God promising him that his numerous descendants will be a blessing to all people (28:14). In the morning, Jacob wakes with a renewed sense of commitment to his purpose and a renewed faith in his covenant with God. He uses just a single stone to mark his purpose, but one is enough. It stands as a sign, a marker of his determination henceforth to trust in God and to walk in his ways. It marks a turning point, the beginning of a new way of thinking and living. From now on, he will not only acknowledge that everything he has and is comes from God, but he will also work to give back to God one-tenth of his possessions.

We too can commit ourselves to living in a way that acknowledges that our talents and our possessions do not belong to us alone but are part of our ongoing relationship with God. As such, they should be shared with the people around us, in God's name.

---

*Generous God, let the cairn we build today be one of generosity, conscious that everything we are and everything we have is a gift from you.*

SALLY WELCH

# A sign of care

Laban said, 'This heap is a witness between you and me today.' Therefore he called it Galeed, and the pillar Mizpah, for he said, 'The Lord watch between you and me, when we are absent one from the other. If you ill-treat my daughters, or if you take wives in addition to my daughters, though no one else is with us, remember that God is witness between you and me.' Then Laban said to Jacob, 'See this heap and see the pillar, which I have set between you and me. This heap is a witness, and the pillar is a witness, that I will not pass beyond this heap to you, and you will not pass beyond this heap and this pillar to me, for harm. May the God of Abraham and the God of Nahor'—the God of their father—'judge between us.' So Jacob swore by the Fear of his father Isaac, and Jacob offered a sacrifice on the height and called his kinsfolk to eat bread; and they ate bread and tarried all night in the hill country.

Laban and Jacob have reached a parting of the ways. It is time for Jacob to leave Laban's household and set up his own establishment with his wives and children. But Laban is still anxious about his daughters' welfare and needs to reassure himself about their future by reminding Jacob of the obligation he owes to them and to Laban. The heap of stones that Jacob and Laban build together, and share a meal around, is a border post, beyond which it is agreed that Jacob will not try to enlarge his territory.

However, it is more than that, for it serves also as a physical sign of a moral agreement. Just as, today, wedding rings mark the commitment of a couple to care for the welfare of each other as tenderly as they care for their own, so the stones mark Jacob's pledge to care for Leah, Rachel and their children.

---

*Use small stones to build a cairn, each stone representing a person in your life whom you are pledged to care for. Pray for their well-being and for yourself, that you may continue faithfully with your obligation to them.*

SALLY WELCH

# God's commitment

[Moses said] On the day that you cross over the Jordan into the land that the Lord your God is giving you, you shall set up large stones and cover them with plaster. You shall write on them all the words of this law when you have crossed over, to enter the land that the Lord your God is giving you, a land flowing with milk and honey, as the Lord, the God of your ancestors, promised you… You must build the altar of the Lord your God of unhewn stones. Then offer up burnt-offerings on it to the Lord your God, make sacrifices of well-being, and eat them there, rejoicing before the Lord your God.

The story of the Old Testament is a story of God's covenant with his children, and his continuing, patient reaffirmation of this covenant in the face of his children's errant behaviour and disobedience. The ten commandments and further instructions—the law given by God—are the means by which the people of Israel will live out their part of the covenant. More than that, they comprise part of the promise of God that he will never abandon them and that he will lead them to their own land, which has been set aside for them, in the future. So the law must be taken seriously and lived out properly, as it holds within it the means by which the people of God will attain their rightful inheritance. When the promise is finally fulfilled, the law will be properly honoured and will continue to be obeyed.

For Christians, the covenant of God finds its fulfilment in the person of Christ, who fulfils all God's promises and provides the path for us to enter into the promised land. Perhaps our church buildings, with all their beauty and dignity, their costliness and size, serve as our declaration of trust in the promises of Christ. They represent our willingness to keep his commandments and to live in the hope of entering his kingdom, providing a place where we can gather to remember his saving actions and our place as God's children.

---

*Does our attitude to our church buildings change if we view them in this light?*

SALLY WELCH

# Let your children know

The people came up out of the Jordan on the tenth day of the first month, and they camped in Gilgal on the eastern border of Jericho. Those twelve stones, which they had taken out of the Jordan, Joshua set up in Gilgal, saying to the Israelites, 'When your children ask their parents in time to come, "What do these stones mean?" then you shall let your children know, "Israel crossed over the Jordan here on dry ground." For the Lord your God dried up the waters of the Jordan for you until you crossed over, as the Lord your God did to the Red Sea, which he dried up for us until we crossed over, so that all the peoples of the earth may know that the hand of the Lord is mighty, and so that you may fear the Lord your God for ever.'

The pilgrim route to Santiago in Spain is dotted with cairns. Some are modest heaps, but others are huge structures, towering over the pilgrims who pause to add another stone to the pile. Although some people simply collect a rock from the wayside to add to the pile, other stones have accompanied the pilgrims from the beginning of their journey, kept safe, with their purpose already identified. These stones are silent witnesses to the millions of people who have walked the route, each with their own hopes and dreams but all aiming for the same destination.

Joshua too builds a pile of stones as a sign that the people of Israel have finally crossed the River Jordan, the target of their desires for so long, marking the place where a new phase of their journey has begun. The stones have been collected from the middle of the River Jordan, that seemingly impenetrable barrier between the people of Israel and their destiny. The river was made safe for crossing by God alone, and in trust the people passed over the dry riverbed to the other side. These stones represent the story of God's saving action, and Joshua and his people commit themselves to telling this story to the children who follow after them.

---

*Father, let the memories of your saving actions be as cairns in our hearts, signs to depend on as we journey into the future.*

SALLY WELCH

# Signs for ourselves

Set up road markers for yourself, make yourself signposts; consider well the highway, the road by which you went. Return, O virgin Israel, return to these your cities.

We had been walking all day in the mountains of Sicily in thick fog, with an unreliable local map. We paused at a crossroads and I remarked to myself that this was the second signpost I had seen with a pile of old road-mending equipment at its base. Then, with a jolt, I realised that this was the same pile and we had travelled in a circle. Having discovered this, we could recalculate and continue on the right path, grateful for the silent help at the signpost.

The prophet Jeremiah, himself a wanderer among many lands and a long-term exile, recognises the value of leaving signs along the way, so that the path home is clearly marked for us if we need it. But these signs are not simply an aid for physical travel. They mark the road to the promised land, the spiritual home of the children of Israel.

Sometimes our lives go off course without us even realising it, and it is not until we have travelled a long way down the wrong track that we pause to take stock of our situation. Realising that we have taken a wrong direction is one thing; discovering the true path to follow is another challenge altogether, and we may feel that we are lost in a wilderness of bad decisions and poor choices. Then we can be grateful for the signs we set down for ourselves in more righteous times—faithful friends, a supportive church, well-loved books and remembered practices. By taking up these habits once more, we will find our true direction, the path intended by God for us to follow.

---

*Pray: Heavenly Father, we know that our true home is with you. Help us to build habits of prayer, friendship, study and praise, so that if we stray, the way home will be clearly signposted. Reflect: If you made a cairn from stones representing the blessings you have received from God, how big would it be?*

SALLY WELCH

# A living stone

Jesus said to them, 'Have you never read in the scriptures: "The stone that the builders rejected has become the cornerstone; this was the Lord's doing, and it is amazing in our eyes"'?

The pathway through the Old Testament is marked with stones—stone altars, memorials to loved ones, signposts and, most significantly, the stone tablets on which God wrote for Moses and his people the laws which they were to follow as children of Israel. These tablets were the spiritual marker stones of the nation. As they travelled on their journey to the promised land, the stones were taken with them as a physical reminder of God's covenant with them.

For Christians, Jesus is the fulfilment of this covenant; he is the promised land in which all who seek may find a home. The cold, harsh stone of the commandments has become the living flesh and blood of Christ, born to take our sins upon him so that we might be set free from our human bondage. 'For Christ is the end of the law so that there may be righteousness for everyone who believes' (Romans 10:4). We no longer have to follow laws inscribed on stone tablets, but instead we have a living example of the lives we are to lead—lives that are concerned with justice and righteousness for all; lives that show mercy and are committed to humble service; lives that, above all, are filled with love for God and for each other.

Isaiah foretold the coming of the Messiah in this way as a 'precious cornerstone, a sure foundation' (Isaiah 28:16), and it is to this that Jesus himself refers. He is the first stone upon which we can build the cairn of our trust in God and our relationship with him. He is the signpost that will guide our feet safely along the path until we can reach our true home.

---

*Lord God, you sent your Son among us to show us, by his example, how to live. Help us to build our lives on the cornerstone of his saving love, that they may be filled with righteousness.*

SALLY WELCH

# Living stones

Come to him, a living stone, though rejected by mortals yet chosen and precious in God's sight, and like living stones, let yourselves be built into a spiritual house, to be a holy priesthood, to offer spiritual sacrifices acceptable to God through Jesus Christ. For it stands in scripture: 'See, I am laying in Zion a stone, a cornerstone chosen and precious; and whoever believes in him will not be put to shame.'

We have seen that Jesus referred to himself as the cornerstone on which God's kingdom would be built. Now he invites us to join in that process. Taking Jesus as our foundation, we are to come together, bringing our whole selves, our gifts and talents, our weaknesses and flaws, and allow ourselves to be built into a 'spiritual house'. No longer 'strangers and aliens', we will become 'citizens with the saints' (Ephesians 2:19) as we are formed into a holy temple, the symbol of God's saving work on earth. We offer 'spiritual sacrifices' to Jesus Christ, the living stone, in direct contrast to those pagans in the Old Testament who were mocked by prophets because they worshipped idols of stone, lifeless objects of no worth or power. The sacrifices that we make are not slaughtered animals, as in former times, but our whole selves, forgiven of our sins by Christ and entering into God's kingdom as a redeemed people.

The concept of the cairn as a waymarker and memorial has been developed even further. Now, the first stone of a new structure, a living stone, has been laid in the person of Christ, and we are being asked to form part of that structure, together with all God's people, to make a new sign in the world, a witness to the work of Christ. We will be changed by these actions into a 'holy priesthood', responding to the work of love achieved in us by Christ, allowing ourselves to be formed into a 'spiritual house'.

---

*Just as a stonemason shapes a stone before using it in a building, so we must be shaped and formed before we can become appropriate material for the house of God. What habits or faults can we try to erase so that this can be accomplished?*

SALLY WELCH

# A new name

Let anyone who has an ear listen to what the Spirit is saying to the churches. To everyone who conquers I will give some of the hidden manna, and I will give a white stone, and on the white stone is written a new name that no one knows except the one who receives it.

At the beginning of the book of Revelation, instructed by Jesus, John writes letters to seven churches. Here, he is writing to the Christians of Pergamum, a city which was the centre for the worship of the pagan gods Zeus, Athene, Dionysus and Asklepios. How important it was for those who were surrounded by idol worship to remain true to their faith! How easy must it have been to become discouraged and weary from holding fast to their beliefs in the face of so much opposition! John reminds them that they must have courage to overcome their doubts and their weaknesses, and he refers to the manna that was given to the people of Israel to sustain them when they were wandering in the desert, homeless and far from the land that had been promised to them.

Some of the manna was kept in the ark of the covenant as a reminder of these times, and it never spoiled (Exodus 16:31–33). So too will the Christians of Pergamum live for ever. The 'white stone' may be a reference to the precious jewel worn by the high priest in Old Testament times, which had God's name on it, or it may be a sign to the recipient that they have become a new person in Christ.

Once again we are being given the gift of becoming signs of the kingdom, laying ourselves down as living stones to be markers of God's grace in the world. If we can keep faith through our times of darkness and doubting, our reward will be to become one of God's children. More wonderful still, that reward does not have to be earned but has already been gained for us by Christ. We simply have to look out for the signs of his coming, becoming in our turn the waymarks of his love.

---

*Heavenly Father, help us to be signs of your saving love for all people.*

SALLY WELCH

*Overleaf...* Size isn't everything | Reading *New Daylight* in a group | Author profile | Recommended reading | Order and subscription forms

# Size isn't everything

LUCY MOORE

**If this were a dodgy news site on the web, I might titivate your interest with a headline something like, 'She opened a book: you'll never BELIEVE what she saw there!' But we were nonetheless all taken aback by what we read in Bob Jackson's book *What Makes Churches Grow? Vision and practice in effective mission*. Bob is a church growth consultant and former Archdeacon of Lichfield and has been an enthusiast for Messy Church for many years. In his book, he describes Messy Church as 'the biggest single churchgoing growth phenomenon in this country since the rise of Sunday schools and Methodism at the end of the eighteenth century'.**

It's an incredible claim, isn't it? I'm so glad it isn't ours. It raises some interesting questions, such as, what does this growth mean for BRF and what does it mean for churches?

We must reach a tipping point sometime. Nothing can or should keep on growing or it will collapse under its own weight, but at the moment we keep on seeing numerical growth. As you probably know, we invite churches to register their Messy Church on the Directory on www.messychurch.org.uk. This is mostly so that families can find their nearest Messy Church easily; it's also so that we can share resources and news with the leaders, and it also helps us when bishops ask, 'Just how many Messy Churches are there?' You can see exactly how many have registered by looking at the homepage of the website, where the number is automatically updated. (As I glance now, #3240 has been started in Eaglesham in East Kilbride. Hooray!)

I'm conscious, as I write, that even if this article were to be published next week, this figure would already be out of date. By the time you read this, I wonder what number and which exotic location will be on the homepage. The speed of growth and change at the moment is phenomenal. We must try not to take it for granted, but to keep on thanking God for it.

Growth happens on different levels. Numerical growth is exciting, but look at the last throwaway comment in Rachel Hill-Brown's recent email:

*I wanted to tell you about our Easter Messy Church. We meet monthly on the second Sunday at 3.30 pm usually and get about 180 people coming… This month we did an extra Messy Church on Maundy Thursday at 10.00 am (first day of school holidays). I had no idea how many to expect but anticipated lower numbers—we had to close the doors when we hit 250 and turned about 30 people away! That felt awful but we were simply full to bursting and any more bodies would have made it unsafe. There were tears! Thankfully we had some balloons to give away, which helped to soften the blow… It was an incredible opportunity to share the Easter story with a whole load of people we don't usually see as well as some regulars. (Oh, and we have more baptism requests too!)*

The growth is encouraging and affirming for us as an organisation. The fact that God chose BRF out of all the mission agencies and ministry groups to be the home for Messy Church is something we relish, across all the BRF teams, in and out of the office. The prayers of so many faithful people over so many years since 1922, when BRF began, have made it a fertile vegetable patch for this particular seed to fall into. We feel very blessed to have been given the privilege of nurturing this little sprout as God makes it grow. It's fantastic to be able to create top-quality books and websites and to run social media accounts through the skills of the wider BRF team.

The growth has given us friends and contacts across the world. As Messy Church has popped up in more than 30 countries, as diverse as Canada and Slovenia, New Zealand and Switzerland, we have chatted on Skype, emailed, and welcomed to our homes and to BRF people from many of those countries. We won't forget giggling with the Icelandic pair, or sharing cake with the women from Holland, or advising the pastor from Norway that it might take a little longer than 30 minutes to get from Hampshire to Heathrow on the M3. And on trips overseas, I have met so many ex-pats who say, 'I've read BRF daily notes for the last 50 years and I've been praying for you ever since you joined BRF.' The spread of Messy Church has meant a reinforcement of BRF links across the globe and a deep sense of joy in those friendships. Bjarne Gertz Olsen emailed only today from Denmark: 'Thank you for your Newsletters as I receive. It's so nice to read about what happen in the Messy Church movement. It's really a blessing. And so great to see how Messy Church now is an International movement. It's great.'

However, it becomes increasingly difficult to support the growing network properly. We only have one Jane Leadbetter to support the 95 Regional Coordinators. If Jane was slapdash, this might be OK, but she sees it as her responsibility to pray for them, pastor them (albeit at a distance) and be there for them, for any and every Messy query or moment of triumph. And 95 people need a great deal of support.

Martyn Payne visits Messy Churches to encourage, learn from and advise them, and to highlight to us what issues are being raised across the country. With the best will in the world, Martyn can only take so many fish fingers a week. Most Messy Churches have to be left to get on with it on their own without personal input from BRF.

I try to make sure church gatekeepers like bishops or District Chairs are happy with what's going on in Messy Churches in their denominations, but time is limited and there are (joyfully!) so many denominations involved: how do we listen to the needs and concerns of all 20-plus?

So growth brings joys but also issues for BRF. How do we ensure that Messy Churches are effectively supported without expanding the BRF Messy team into an unwieldy crowd, needing even more admin and structures to make it work, and for which we don't have funding in any case? How do we ensure that we are the wise accompaniers of Messy leaders, not corks in the bottle through lack of resources?

On a bigger scale, what are the denominations going to do about this growth phenomenon in their midst? Will the impressive stats mean that clergy training is altered to help church leaders make the most of the opportunities in the Messy Churches for which they are responsible? Will they help BRF with the constant need for core funding? Will they draw Messy Church strategically into their growth plans? Will they affirm the ministry of lay leaders within the churches? Will they listen to what this rather scruffy angel is saying to the churches about what families this century need from their local church? Or will they politely ignore it and wait for it to go away?

'I planted the seed, Apollos watered it, but God has been making it grow' (1 Corinthians 3:6). If this is God's hand at work, we can only trust that God will grow this strange and messy family in the way that he knows is best.

*Lucy Moore is the founder and team leader of BRF's Messy Church.*

# Reading *New Daylight* in a group

SALLY WELCH

**I am aware that although some of you cherish the moments of quiet during the day that enable you to read and reflect on the passages we offer you in *New Daylight*, other readers prefer to study in small groups, to enable conversation and discussion and the sharing of insights. With this in mind, here are some ideas for discussion starters within a study group. Some of the questions are generic and can be applied to any set of contributions within this issue; others are specific to certain sets of readings. I hope they generate some interesting reflections and conversations.**

## General discussion starters

These questions can be used for any study series within this issue. Remember, there are no right or wrong answers; they are intended simply to enable a group to engage in conversation.

- What do you think is the main idea or theme of the author in this series? Do you think the writer succeeded in communicating this idea to you, or were you more interested in the side issues?
- Have you had any experience of the issues that are raised in the study? How have they affected your life?
- What evidence does the author use to support their ideas? Do they use personal observations and experience, facts, or quotations from other authorities? Which appeals to you most?
- Does the author make a 'call to action'? Is that call realistic and achievable? Do you think their ideas will work in the secular world?
- Can you identify specific passages that struck you personally—as interesting, profound, difficult to understand or illuminating?
- Did you learn something new from reading this series? Will you think differently about some things, and if so, what are they?

## Atonement (Veronica Zundel)

- In her contributions for this issue, Veronica explores different approaches to the atonement of Christ. Which of these do you find most appealing? Which of them challenge you? In what ways has this set of reflections helped you to understand your faith?

**Anger (David Winter)**

Anger can sometimes be seen as a dangerous emotion, but are there times when you think anger is justified? Do you agree with David's analysis of these times in his examples? How has your understanding of the purpose of God's anger developed through these readings?

**Reflective question: Cairns (Sally Welch)**

In this study of the use of cairns in the Bible, Sally reflects on the way cairns are built to commemorate a place where God has acted to bless his people.

What blessings has God given you for your journey?

# Author profile: Naomi Starkey

**Revd Naomi Starkey** is well known to long-term *New Daylight* readers. Editor **Sally Welch** asked her to talk about her work and her writing.

*Naomi, you are not a new writer to* New Daylight, *but your job has changed. Can you tell us what you do now?*

I write this sitting at my study window in a vicarage in north-west Wales, dog collar in place ready for a church meeting this evening. Until June 2015, I was a commissioning editor for BRF, a job that, over 18 years, involved editing books, *New Daylight* and *Quiet Spaces*, as well as doing my own writing. I worked mostly from home, but my whole pattern of life, as well as location, have undergone huge changes over the past few years.

*How have you found the change?*

I had known other women who felt called to church ministry when family commitments began to change, but never expected to be one such myself. Having said that, I love my role as curate in a team that covers six churches, including two that are Welsh-speaking only. No, I am not Welsh—and, yes, I learned the language, starting with evening classes back in January 2010.

*You live and work in Bro Enlli. What is that like?*

One downside of life in a 'deep rural' area is the amount of driving involved, but that is more than compensated for by easy access to beautiful beaches and, a bit further afield, the dramatic landscapes of Snowdonia. I have found it fascinating to get to know the very different rhythms of life in summer and winter.

*How do you fit in your writing?*

With preparing sermons each week (often in two languages), time for my own writing can start to feel squeezed. Before I embarked on church ministry, though, a friend told me about the importance of building 'islands' in the 'river' of the week—opportunities to recharge, focus on hobbies, and so on. If I am not careful, such 'islands' can end up in danger of being eroded, and working to avoid that is part of the discipline involved for me in continuing to grow in this new way of life.

# Recommended reading

BRF's 2017 Lent book is by **Amy Boucher Pye**, who will be familiar to readers of *New Daylight* and *Day by Day with God* notes. Moving from Ash Wednesday to Easter Day, daily reflections and prayers help us to experience the living power of the cross of Christ through biblical and modern-day stories of wrongdoing and forgiveness. The following extract is from the beginning of the book.

**Fallen Heroes: the Israelite Founders**

In our journey of exploring the living cross as the source of forgiveness and new life, we start on Ash Wednesday at the very beginning, when it all goes wrong as Adam and Eve turn from God. From the start, we see our need for a Saviour, for Jesus to become the new Adam who leads us into life eternal.

We move next to sibling relationships and sibling rivalry, a tearing-apart between brothers that unfortunately continues through the generations, reflecting our need for Jesus' work on the cross. Then we come to our first fallen-but-redeemed founders of the faith, Abram and Sarai, who act on their fears through deception (Abram) and by turning to their own ways of making things happen (Sarai) instead of trusting God. Yet the Lord saves them and fulfils his promises, just as he made good on saving us from the curse of the law.

We encounter more sibling strife with Jacob and Esau, including parents who favour one child over the other and the destruction that follows. And yet God's redemptive work in Jacob brings harmony and reconciliation, hinting at the restored relationships we enjoy at the foot of the cross. Yet more unhappy families greet us in the stories of Joseph and his brothers, but we see also how God redeems the sin and deceit, as Joseph saves his family and God's people from destruction through famine. So too does Jesus save us.

Our extended week ends with Moses, another great leader of God's people. He is a murderer, yet is used by God as his instrument to lead his people to the promised land. We, like Moses, are made new at the living cross, where we can leave behind the old self as we put on the clothes of the new.

## Ash Wednesday: First sins

*Now the snake was more crafty than any of the wild animals the Lord God had made. He said to the woman, 'Did God really say, "You must not eat from any tree in the garden"?'*

*The woman said to the snake, 'We may eat fruit from the trees in the garden, but God did say, "You must not eat fruit from the tree that is in the middle of the garden, and you must not touch it, or you will die."'*

*'You will not certainly die,' the snake said to the woman. 'For God knows that when you eat from it your eyes will be opened, and you will be like God, knowing good and evil.'*

*When the woman saw that the fruit of the tree was good for food and pleasing to the eye, and also desirable for gaining wisdom, she took some and ate it. She also gave some to her husband, who was with her, and he ate it. Then the eyes of both of them were opened, and they realised they were naked; so they sewed fig leaves together and made coverings for themselves.*

GENESIS 3:1–7 (NIV)

They take and eat, and life will never be the same again.

Adam and Eve's eyes open after eating from the tree of the knowledge of good and evil, and they know more than God intends them—and us—to know. Though the fruit looks pleasing, consuming it results in the worst stomach ache ever. But they are not left in the garden alone, helpless and hopeless, for the Lord God loves them and enacts a remedy—his grand rescue plan.

We start our Lenten journey of exploring the gift of forgiveness and new life with the fall of humanity, for when our first parents disobey God, the world changes for ever. This side of heaven, never again will we live in complete peace and harmony. Never again will we enjoy shame-free communion with our Maker or each other. Never again will we fully escape wrongful desire, severe labour or painful toil. We need the grace that God's forgiveness imparts.

Thus we need a Saviour, for Adam and Eve's turning from God ushers in repeat performances of disobedience down the ages, starting with their own duelling sons and continuing through the daughters and sons to follow: Abraham, Isaac, Jacob, Joseph, Moses and so on. They are heroes of our faith, but imperfect ones. For instance, in fear Abraham passes off his wife as his sister; Isaac favours one son over another; Jacob steals his brother's rightful blessing; Joseph lords his special position over his brothers; and Moses wrongfully kills an Egyptian. The list continues.

But God in his gracious mercy provides the solution to our dilemma: he sends his only Son to die in our place, redeeming us from the curse of the law (see Galatians 3:10–14). No longer do we need to be separated from God through our sins and wrongdoing, but can be restored to a right relationship with him through Jesus' sacrifice. The cross is therefore a living place of exchange: the blood of Jesus removes the stain of our wrongdoing and imparts to us freedom and new life.

Although we are forgiven, we still need to forgive and be forgiven by others. At the cross we can name our wrongful behaviour and impure thoughts and ask for God's forgiveness. As we confess our sins, one by one, God will forgive us and bring us freedom. And there we can take those wrongs committed against us, that they may no longer hold and shape us.

As we embark on exploring biblical stories of wrongs committed and forgiveness bestowed, may we grow in love for the triune God—Father, Son and Holy Spirit. May our journey to the cross and resurrection bestow on us an abiding sense of faith, hope and love. And may the spiritual disciplines we undertake during this journey bring about in us a renewed sense of wonder and gratitude for Jesus' great gift of death and new life: 'For as in Adam all die, so in Christ all will be made alive' (1 Corinthians 15:22).

### Prayer

*Loving Lord, the world is not as you created it. When Adam and Eve turned their faces from you in disobedience, sin and sickness entered in. But you sent your Son to die in my place, moving me from a place of death to new life. Please strengthen my understanding of and love for you during this grace-filled journey. In your time, reveal the areas where I need to relinquish control or confess my wrongdoing. I am humbled by your sacrifice, Lord Jesus. Thank you for making me clean.*

To order a copy of this book, please turn to the order form on page 149.

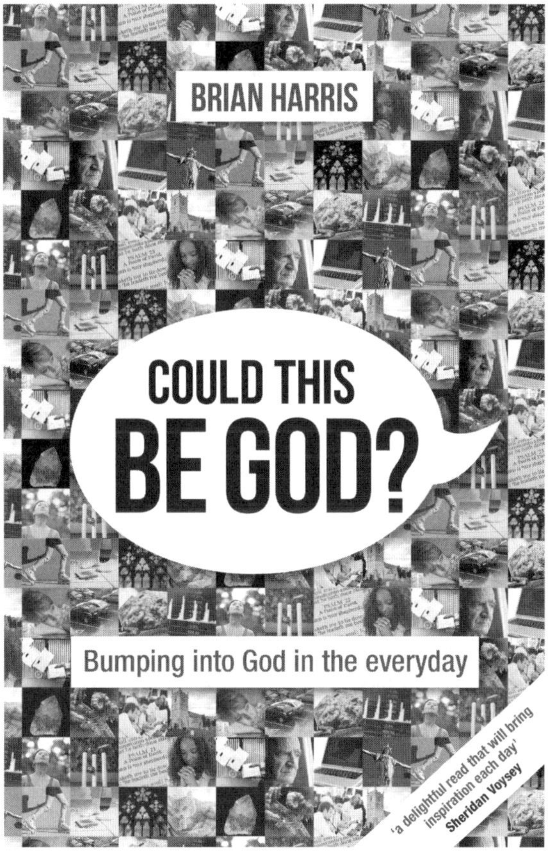
BRIAN HARRIS
COULD THIS
BE GOD?
Bumping into God in the everyday
'a delightful read that will bring inspiration each day'
Sheridan Voysey

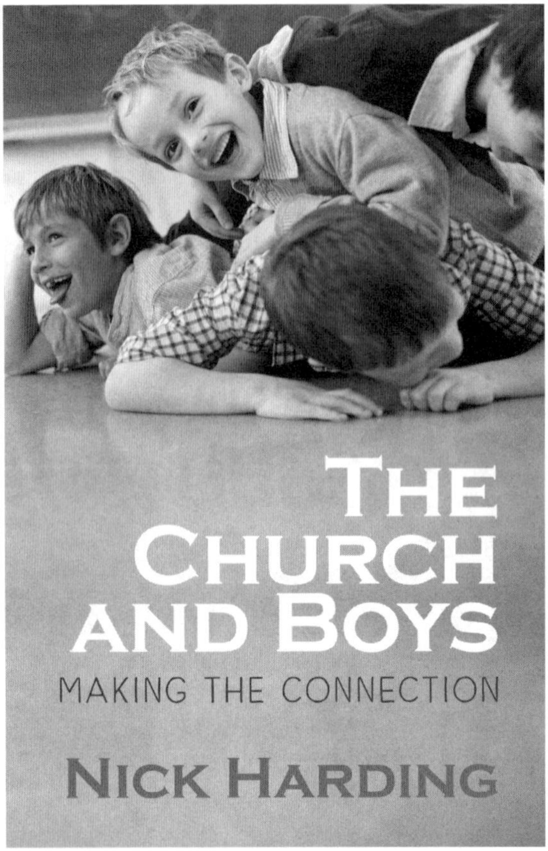


Why are boys so under-represented in churches? Why do churches find it so difficult to cater for boys? What would help boys in church grow into mature men of faith? This uniquely inspiring book spells out the problem and encourages churches to see it in missional terms. The book includes resources, suggestions and ideas to help boys connect better with the church, with the Bible, and with the Christian faith.

**The Church and Boys**
*Making the connection*
Nick Harding
978 0 85746 509 2 £8.99
brf.org.uk

# To order

Online: **brfonline.org.uk**
Telephone: +44 (0)1865 319700
Mon–Fri 9.15–17.30

Delivery times within the UK are normally 15 working days. Prices are correct at the time of going to press but may change without prior notice.

| Title | Price | Qty | Total |
|---|---|---|---|
| The Living Cross | £8.99 | | |
| Spiritual Growth in a Time of Change | £7.99 | | |
| Stepping into Grace | £7.99 | | |
| Could This Be God? | £8.99 | | |
| The Church and Boys | £8.99 | | |
| The Recovery of Hope | £8.99 | | |
| Mary | £8.99 | | |
| Everything I Know About God… | £7.99 | | |
| Heaven's Morning | £7.99 | | |

| POSTAGE AND PACKING CHARGES | | | |
|---|---|---|---|
| **Order value** | **UK** | **Europe** | **Rest of world** |
| Under £7.00 | £1.25 | £3.00 | £5.50 |
| £7.00–£29.99 | £2.25 | £5.50 | £10.00 |
| £30.00 and over | FREE | Prices on request | |

| | |
|---|---|
| Total value of books | |
| Postage and packing | |
| Total for this order | |

**Please complete in BLOCK CAPITALS**

Title .......... First name/initials .................. Surname ..............................

Address ..............................................................

...................................................... Postcode ....................

Acc. No. .............................. Telephone ..............................

Email ..............................................................

Please keep me informed about BRF's books and resources ❑ by email ❑ by post
Please keep me informed about the wider work of BRF ❑ by email ❑ by post

## Method of payment

❑ Cheque (made payable to BRF) ❑ MasterCard / Visa

Card no. ☐☐☐☐ ☐☐☐☐ ☐☐☐☐ ☐☐☐☐

Valid from ☐☐ ☐☐ Expires ☐☐ ☐☐ Security code* ☐☐☐
Last 3 digits on the reverse of the card

Signature* .................................................. Date ......../......../........

*ESSENTIAL IN ORDER TO PROCESS YOUR ORDER

**Please return this form to:** BRF, 15 The Chambers, Vineyard, Abingdon OX14 3FE | enquiries@brf.org.uk
To read our terms and find out about cancelling your order, please visit **brfonline.org.uk/terms**.

The Bible Reading Fellowship (BRF) is a Registered Charity (233280)

# How to encourage Bible reading in your church

BRF has been helping individuals connect with the Bible for over 90 years. We want to support churches as they seek to encourage church members into regular Bible reading.

### Order a Bible reading resources pack

This pack is designed to give your church the tools to publicise our Bible reading notes. It includes:

- Sample Bible reading notes for your congregation to try.
- Publicity resources, including a poster.
- A church magazine feature about Bible reading notes.

The pack is free, but we welcome a £5 donation to cover the cost of postage. If you require a pack to be sent outside the UK or require a specific number of sample Bible reading notes, please contact us for postage costs. More information about what the current pack contains is available on our website.

### How to order and find out more

- Visit **biblereadingnotes.org.uk/for-churches**
- Telephone BRF on +44 (0)1865 319700 Mon–Fri 9.15–17.30
- Write to us at BRF, 15 The Chambers, Vineyard, Abingdon OX14 3FE

### Keep informed about our latest initiatives

We are continuing to develop resources to help churches encourage people into regular Bible reading, wherever they are on their journey. Join our email list at **biblereadingnotes.org.uk/helpingchurches** to stay informed about the latest initiatives that your church could benefit from.

### Introduce a friend to our notes

We can send information about our notes and current prices for you to pass on. Please contact us.

# Transforming Lives and Communities

BRF is a charity that is passionate about making a difference through the Christian faith. We want to see lives and communities transformed through our creative programmes and resources for individuals, churches and schools. We are doing this by resourcing:

- **Christian growth and understanding of the Bible.** Through our Bible reading notes, books, digital resources, Quiet Days and other events, we're resourcing individuals, groups and leaders in churches for their own spiritual journey and for their ministry.
- **Church outreach in the local community.** BRF is the home of three programmes that churches are embracing to great effect as they seek to engage with their local communities: Messy Church, Who Let The Dads Out? and The Gift of Years.
- **Teaching Christianity in primary schools.** Our Barnabas in Schools team is working with primary-aged children and their teachers, enabling them to explore Christianity creatively within the school curriculum.
- **Children's and family ministry.** Through our Barnabas in Churches and Faith in Homes websites and published resources, we're working with churches and families, enabling children under 11, and the adults working with them, to explore Christianity creatively and bring the Bible alive.

## Do you share our vision?

Sales of our books and Bible reading notes cover the cost of producing them. However, our other programmes are funded primarily by donations, grants and legacies. If you share our vision, would you help us to transform even more lives and communities? Your prayers and financial support are vital for the work that we do.

- You could support BRF's ministry with a one-off gift or regular donation (using the response form on page 153).
- You could consider making a bequest to BRF in your will (page 152).
- You could encourage your church to support BRF as part of your church's giving to home mission—perhaps focusing on a specific area of our ministry, or a particular member of our Barnabas team.
- Most important of all, you could support BRF with your prayers.

# Make a lasting difference through a gift in your will

BRF's story began almost a century ago when a vicar in Brixton, south London, introduced daily Bible readings to help his congregation 'get a move on spiritually'. Today our creative programmes and resources impact thousands of lives and communities across the UK and worldwide, from Brixton to Brisbane.

One such programme is **Who Let The Dads Out?**, which is working to transform family relationships in the UK by turning the hearts of fathers to their children and the hearts of children to their fathers (Malachi 4:6). The relationship between father and child is spiritually significant, and when you lead a father from a non-Christian family to Christ there is a 93 per cent probability that the family will follow. Who Let The Dads Out? is making ready a people prepared for the Lord and causing a cultural shift, encouraging churches to value and invest in ministry to fathers.

If you share our passion for making a difference through the Christian faith, please consider leaving a gift in your will to BRF. Gifts in wills are an important source of income for us and they don't need to be huge to make a real difference. For every £1 you give, we will invest 88p back into charitable activities. Just imagine what we could do over the next century with your help.

For further information about making a gift to BRF in your will, please visit **brf.org.uk** or contact Sophie on 01865 319700 or email giving@brf.org.uk.

**Whatever you can do or give, we thank you for your support.**

## SHARING OUR VISION – MAKING A GIFT

**I would like to make a gift to support BRF. Please use my gift for:**

☐ where it is needed most ☐ Barnabas Children's Ministry

☐ Messy Church ☐ Who Let The Dads Out? ☐ The Gift of Years

Title | First name/initials | Surname

Address

Postcode

Email

Telephone

Signature | Date

*giftaid it* You can add an extra 25p to every £1 you give.

**Please treat as Gift Aid donations all qualifying gifts of money made**

☐ today, ☐ in the past four years, ☐ and in the future.

I am a UK taxpayer and understand that if I pay less Income Tax and/or Capital Gains Tax in the current tax year than the amount of Gift Aid claimed on all my donations, it is my responsibility to pay any difference.

☐ My donation does not qualify for Gift Aid.

Please notify BRF if you want to cancel this Gift Aid declaration, change your name or home address, or no longer pay sufficient tax on your income and/or capital gains.

Please complete other side of form ➲

**Please return this form to:**

BRF, 15 The Chambers, Vineyard, Abingdon OX14 3FE

BRF

The Bible Reading Fellowship is a Registered Charity (233280)

## SHARING OUR VISION – MAKING A GIFT

### Regular giving

By Direct Debit:

☐ I would like to make a regular gift of £ ☐ per month/quarter/year.
Please also complete the Direct Debit instruction on page 159.

By Standing Order:

Please contact Priscilla Kew, tel. +44 (0)1235 462305; giving@brf.org.uk

### One-off donation

Please accept my gift of:

☐ £10 ☐ £50 ☐ £100 Other £ ☐

by (delete as appropriate):

☐ Cheque/Charity Voucher payable to 'BRF'

☐ MasterCard/Visa/Debit card/Charity card

Name on card

Card no. ☐☐☐☐ ☐☐☐☐ ☐☐☐☐ ☐☐☐☐

Valid from M M Y Y Expires M M Y Y

Security code* ☐☐☐ *Last 3 digits on the reverse of the card
ESSENTIAL IN ORDER TO PROCESS YOUR PAYMENT

Signature | Date

We like to acknowledge all donations. However, if you do not wish to receive an acknowledgement, please tick here ☐

Please complete other side of form

**Please return this form to:**

BRF, 15 The Chambers, Vineyard, Abingdon OX14 3FE

BRF

## NEW DAYLIGHT SUBSCRIPTION RATES

Please note our new subscription rates for the coming year. From the May 2017 issue, the new subscription rates will be:

### Individual subscriptions

covering 3 issues for under 5 copies, payable in advance (including postage & packing):

| | UK | Europe | Rest of world |
|---|---|---|---|
| *New Daylight* | £16.50 | £24.60 | £28.50 |
| *New Daylight*<br>3-year subscription (9 issues)<br>(not available for Deluxe) | £45.00 | N/A | N/A |
| *New Daylight Deluxe*<br>per set of 3 issues p.a. | £20.85 | £33.45 | £40.50 |

### Group subscriptions

covering 3 issues for 5 copies or more, sent to **one** UK address (post free):

| | |
|---|---|
| *New Daylight* | £13.20 per set of 3 issues p.a. |
| *New Daylight Deluxe* | £16.95 per set of 3 issues p.a. |

Please note that the annual billing period for group subscriptions runs from 1 May to 30 April.

### Overseas group subscription rates

Available on request. Please email enquiries@brf.org.uk.

Copies may also be obtained from Christian bookshops:

| | |
|---|---|
| *New Daylight* | £4.40 per copy |
| *New Daylight Deluxe* | £5.65 per copy |

All our Bible reading notes can be ordered online by visiting **biblereadingnotes.org.uk/subscriptions**

For information about our other Bible reading notes, and apps for iPhone and iPod touch, visit **biblereadingnotes.org.uk**

# NEW DAYLIGHT INDIVIDUAL SUBSCRIPTION FORM

All our Bible reading notes can be ordered online by visiting
**biblereadingnotes.org.uk/subscriptions**

☐ I would like to take out a subscription:

Title ........... First name/initials .............. Surname ....................................

Address .....................................................................................

............................................................ Postcode ........................

Telephone ............................ Email .............................................

Please send *New Daylight* beginning with the May 2017 / September 2017 / January 2018 issue (*delete as appropriate*):

| (*please tick box*) | UK | Europe | Rest of world |
|---|---|---|---|
| *New Daylight* | ☐ £16.50 | ☐ £24.60 | ☐ £28.50 |
| *New Daylight* 3-year subscription | ☐ £45.00 | N/A | N/A |
| *New Daylight Deluxe* | ☐ £20.85 | ☐ £33.45 | ☐ £40.50 |

Total enclosed £ .................. (cheques should be made payable to 'BRF')

Please charge my MasterCard / Visa ☐ Debit card ☐ with £ ................

Card no. ☐☐☐☐ ☐☐☐☐ ☐☐☐☐ ☐☐☐☐

Valid from M M Y Y Expires M M Y Y Security code* ☐☐☐

Last 3 digits on the reverse of the card

Signature* ........................................................ Date ....../....../......

*ESSENTIAL IN ORDER TO PROCESS YOUR PAYMENT

To set up a Direct Debit, please also complete the Direct Debit instruction on page 159 and return it to BRF with this form.

**Please return this form with the appropriate payment to:**
BRF, 15 The Chambers, Vineyard, Abingdon OX14 3FE

To read our terms and find out about cancelling your order, please visit **brfonline.org.uk/terms**.

The Bible Reading Fellowship (BRF) is a Registered Charity (233280)



ND0117

# NEW DAYLIGHT GIFT SUBSCRIPTION FORM

☐ I would like to give a gift subscription (please provide both names and addresses):

Title ............ First name/initials .............. Surname ........................................

Address ........................................................................................

.......................................................................... Postcode ........................

Telephone ........................... Email ........................................................

Gift subscription name ..........................................................................

Gift subscription address .......................................................................

.......................................................................... Postcode ........................

Gift message (20 words max. or include your own gift card):

..................................................................................................

..................................................................................................

Please send *New Daylight* beginning with the May 2017 / September 2017 / January 2018 issue (*delete as appropriate*):

| (*please tick box*) | UK | Europe | Rest of world |
|---|---|---|---|
| *New Daylight* | ☐ £16.50 | ☐ £24.60 | ☐ £28.50 |
| *New Daylight* 3-year subscription | ☐ £45.00 | N/A | N/A |
| *New Daylight Deluxe* | ☐ £20.85 | ☐ £33.45 | ☐ £40.50 |

Total enclosed £ .................. (cheques should be made payable to 'BRF')

Please charge my MasterCard / Visa ☐ Debit card ☐ with £ ..................

Card no. ☐☐☐☐ ☐☐☐☐ ☐☐☐☐ ☐☐☐☐

Valid from ☐☐ ☐☐ Expires ☐☐ ☐☐ Security code* ☐☐☐

Last 3 digits on the reverse of the card

Signature* ............................................................ Date ....../....../......

*ESSENTIAL IN ORDER TO PROCESS YOUR PAYMENT

To set up a Direct Debit, please also complete the Direct Debit instruction on page 159 and return it to BRF with this form.

**Please return this form with the appropriate payment to:**
BRF, 15 The Chambers, Vineyard, Abingdon OX14 3FE

BRF

To read our terms and find out about cancelling your order, please visit **brfonline.org.uk/terms**.

The Bible Reading Fellowship (BRF) is a Registered Charity (233280)

# DIRECT DEBIT PAYMENT

You can pay for your annual subscription to our Bible reading notes using Direct Debit. You need only give your bank details once, and the payment is made automatically every year until you cancel it. If you would like to pay by Direct Debit, please use the form opposite, entering your BRF account number under 'Reference number'.

You are fully covered by the Direct Debit Guarantee:

## The Direct Debit Guarantee

- This Guarantee is offered by all banks and building societies that accept instructions to pay Direct Debits.
- If there are any changes to the amount, date or frequency of your Direct Debit, The Bible Reading Fellowship will notify you 10 working days in advance of your account being debited or as otherwise agreed. If you request The Bible Reading Fellowship to collect a payment, confirmation of the amount and date will be given to you at the time of the request.
- If an error is made in the payment of your Direct Debit, by The Bible Reading Fellowship or your bank or building society, you are entitled to a full and immediate refund of the amount paid from your bank or building society.
- If you receive a refund you are not entitled to, you must pay it back when The Bible Reading Fellowship asks you to.
- You can cancel a Direct Debit at any time by simply contacting your bank or building society. Written confirmation may be required. Please also notify us.

The Bible Reading Fellowship

# Instruction to your bank or building society to pay by Direct Debit

DIRECT Debit

Please fill in the whole form using a ballpoint pen and return it to:
BRF, 15 The Chambers, Vineyard, Abingdon OX14 3FE

Service User Number: | 5 | 5 | 8 | 2 | 2 | 9 |

Name and full postal address of your bank or building society

| To: The Manager | Bank/Building Society |
|---|---|
| Address | |
| | |
| | |
| | Postcode |

Name(s) of account holder(s)

| |
|---|
| |

Branch sort code [ ][ ] – [ ][ ] – [ ][ ]

Bank/Building Society account number [ ][ ][ ][ ][ ][ ][ ][ ]

Reference number [ ][ ][ ][ ][ ][ ][ ]

Instruction to your Bank/Building Society

Please pay The Bible Reading Fellowship Direct Debits from the account detailed in this instruction, subject to the safeguards assured by the Direct Debit Guarantee. I understand that this instruction may remain with The Bible Reading Fellowship and, if so, details will be passed electronically to my bank/building society.

| Signature(s) |
|---|
| |

Banks and Building Societies may not accept Direct Debit instructions for some types of account.

This page is left blank for your notes.